NEW — A PREVIOUS

FROM WHITE TF

THE SIMPLICITY OF THE INCARNATION
BY J STAFFORD WRIGHT
Foreword by J I Packer

The Simplicity of the Incarnation

J STAFFORD WRIGHT
FOREWORD BY J. I. PACKER

"I believe in … Jesus Christ … born of the Virgin Mary." A beautiful stained glass image, or a medical reality? This is the choice facing Christians today. Can we truly believe that two thousand years ago a young woman, a virgin named Mary, gave birth to the Son of God? The answer is simple: we can.

The author says, *"In these days many Christians want some sensible assurance that their faith makes sense, and in this book I want to show that it does."*

In this uplifting book from a previously unpublished and recently discovered manuscript, J Stafford Wright investigates the reality of the incarnation, looks at the crucifixion and resurrection of Jesus, and helps the reader understand more of the Trinity and the certainty of eternal life in heaven.

This book was written shortly before the author's death in 1985. *The Simplicity of the Incarnation* is published for the first time, unedited, from his final draft.

ISBN 13: 9-780-9525-9563-2
160 pages 5.25 x 8 inches £7:95 and US $11:95
Available from bookstores and major internet sellers

BIBLE PEOPLE REAL PEOPLE
by J STAFFORD WRIGHT

In a fascinating look at real people, J Stafford Wright shows his love and scholarly knowledge of the Bible as he brings the characters from its pages to life in a memorable way.

- ✓ Read this book through from A to Z, like any other title.
- ✓ Dip in and discover who was who in personal Bible study.
- ✓ Check the names when preparing a talk or sermon.

The good, the bad, the beautiful and the ugly – no one is spared. This is a book for everyone who wants to get to grips with the reality that is in the pages of the Bible, the Word of God.

With the names arranged in alphabetical order, the Old and New Testament characters are clearly identified so that the reader is able to explore either the Old or New Testament people on the first reading, and the other Testament on the second.

Those wanting to become more familiar with the Bible will find this is a great introduction to the people inhabiting the best selling book in the world, and those already familiar with the Bible will find everyone suddenly becomes much more real – because these people *are* real. This is a book to keep handy and refer to frequently while reading the Bible.

ISBN 13: 9-780-9525-9565-6
314 pages 6 x 9 inches £9.95 and US $14.95
Available from bookstores and major internet sellers
Previously published as *Dictionary of Bible People*

MAKES A GREAT GIFT!

CHRISTIANS AND THE SUPERNATURAL

J STAFFORD WRIGHT

Compiled and abridged from *Understanding the Supernatural*
© J Stafford Wright 1977 published by Scripture Union
and from *Our Mysterious God* ©1984 J Stafford Wright
published by Marshall Morgan & Scott

This abridged edition ©2011 C Stafford Wright

ISBN 9-780-9525-9564-9

PUBLISHED BY
WHITE TREE PUBLISHING
28 FALLODON WAY
BRISTOL BS9 4HX
UNITED KINGDOM

To my grandson, Jonathan,
with whom I have discussed these
and other mysteries

Contents

Publisher's Note

White Tree Publishing is privileged to have the opportunity to republish, in this abridged volume, two books by J Stafford Wright – *Understanding the Supernatural*, published in 1977 (which was a revision of *Christianity and the Occult* first published in 1971), and *Our Mysterious God* published in 1984, a year before the author's death.

J Stafford Wright, a renowned evangelical Bible scholar and expert on biblical Hebrew and Greek, carefully selected each Bible quotation from the versions that were then to hand. The sections from *Understanding the Supernatural* quote mainly from the RSV, and the sections from *Our Mysterious God* from the NIV. (The NIV was not published until 1973.)

Because there was material in common between the two titles, some sections have been deleted where there was repetition, and chapters and pages from the two books have been blended together in a new order. This means that there is a mix of RSV and NIV quotes throughout this volume. Where only a few words of a text have been quoted, and these are identical, or nearly identical between the two translations, no attribution has been given.

These versions were selected by the author not to back up theories or ideas that are out of line with other translations, but because in the writer's view the available versions quoted here most accurately portray the exact meaning of the original Greek and Hebrew languages. Our more recent, as well as earlier English Bible translations like the KJV, generally have very similar wording, and can be used with confidence when looking up the Bible references – something that the reader is recommended to do.

About this Book

Is the supernatural necessarily evil? Perhaps surprisingly to some readers, it is not. The Bible clearly teaches that there is a physical *and* an unseen spiritual world – both worlds created by God – surrounding us whether we understand it or not. If this is so, how much notice should we take of the unseen world?

My father, J Stafford Wright wrote the two books, abridged here by me into this single volume, on the Christian's approach to the supernatural and mysterious events. Although they have been out of print for some time, the problems of the occult and supernatural facing Christians today have certainly not gone away, and many critics question whether it is reasonable to accept the Bible miracles as genuine.

In the twenty-first century, interest in the occult is greater than ever. There is a real battle of good against evil, in our world and in our personal lives – not just in the Harry Potter books that draw some criticism for glorifying the occult.

Is it really wrong to try to contact our dead loved ones in a seance? Well, it may be wrong, but surely it cannot be dangerous. What about Tarot cards and fortune-telling? Where is the harm in horoscopes? After all, not many people seriously believe in the Devil. Do they? Be warned, he is real, as the Bible teaches throughout the Old and New Testaments, and he is most definitely believed in by Jesus. In that case, should we be afraid of the Devil and his demons? My father deals with questions like these in this book, showing the reader exactly what the Bible has to say.

A great theologian with a very human side, my father often discussed these matters with me, and later with my son Jonathan who was then in his late teens. We both feel the time is right to let a new generation of readers explore, from a strong Bible-based Christian perspective, what is going on in the spiritual world, and discover the difference between using our untapped abilities for God, and being deceived by the enemy into misusing them.

A couple of the events that my father wrote about have subsequently had more likely explanations, and I have mentioned these in footnotes. One is the Aberfan disaster, where slurry from a coal tip above the Welsh village slid down to cover the school, killing most of the children inside in 1966. As my father writes, nearly eighty people claimed to have dreamt that it would happen, although only three of these people had told anyone of their dream before the event. However, later research has discovered that there had been unease in the village for some time about the stability of this coal tip, which could account for the majority of these dreams.

This is not to say that no dreams foretell the future, because we can see in the Bible that they do, nor is it to say that the Aberfan dreams were of no significance, but we do need to be careful of what we accept if there are other reasonable explanations.

To put the majority of dreams into perspective, let's say for the purpose of illustration that a million people in the world dream about a large passenger plane crash on any one night. No plane crashes, and the dream is either dismissed or forgotten by those million. Then one day there is news of a major airline tragedy. The million people who had the dream that particular night can now say, "I dreamt about that last night!" This, of course, as my father would readily have admitted, proves nothing. To dream about a plane crash *and* a significant detail such as the name of the pilot, *and* tell someone about the dream in advance of the crash, would be very convincing that the dream foretold the future.

Chance is another area that is often misunderstood. I take a packet of loose tea and toss the contents into the air. The tea-leaves land in a pattern on the ground that is clearly that of a rabbit. What are the chances of my action making the shape of a rabbit? A hundred to one, a thousand to one? But hold on, I didn't say I was going to make the shape of a rabbit before I threw the tea-leaves. The question we need to ask is this: what are the chances of the tea-leaves making *any* shape that is recognisable as something? The answer is that they will almost certainly land in some identifiable shape. We need to bear this in mind when considering whether something was controlled by an outside agency, or was just chance; although as we read in this book, God often works and answers prayer through natural circumstances – the miracle being in the timing.

The monthly magazine *Fortean Times*, with occasional lurid covers and some advertisements and articles that many Christians would consider unsuitable for family reading, sets out in a very professional way to research and demolish some dubious accounts of so-called psychic phenomena that have passed into popular belief. Their writers also research other events and find them credible. Careful, unbiased research is needed before accepting or rejecting any reported modern miracle or psychic event.

Word War II Bomber Found on Moon! Newspaper headlines like this are automatically dismissed as harmless, even if over-enthusiastic journalism. *Man Sees Through Glass Eye After Prayer.* This is a serious claim and needs careful investigation before repeating it as fact. We often hear of miracles that can never be traced back to their roots. In the secular world these are called urban myths, such as, "My friend told me that this really weird thing actually happened to her father …" and so on. But when we investigate, it turns out that it didn't happen to your friend's father after all. He says he heard it from a friend at work about *his* father, but that friend says he heard it from another friend, who heard it from another, and so on. So before repeating a miracle as a wonderful example of God overruling in a certain event, we need to know exactly who it happened to, or else repeat it as something we've heard but are unable to verify. Only in this way will accounts of miracles be honouring to God.

Following this line of needing to check everything at source, my father looked into original documents of the prophecies of the sixteenth century French prophet Nostradamus, rather than accepting a version in a modern book. He wanted to verify the wording, since from

Victorian times onward the verses were often changed and even added to in books, with lines that Nostradamus never wrote.

What would he have made of the internet, where many so-called Nostradamus prophecies have been invented or distorted to suit current events, and put online as genuine? In fact, the internet is extremely unreliable when it comes to investigating supernatural or supposedly supernatural events, although it can be useful for finding out more about people involved in the supernatural.

In abridging the two books to make this single volume, no new thoughts have been added or conclusions altered, although some sections have been moved around or cut to make the single volume more coherent, especially where there was repetition in the two originals. I have inserted the occasional wording in square brackets, and added my own footnotes in places to explain some things in a little more detail for twenty-first century readers. So any errors in these are mine. Words in round brackets are from the original, as are footnotes attributed to the author.

Chris Wright

Bristol

2011

1: A Puzzle

Consider the following. One night you wake up and see the form of a friend who is living hundreds of miles away. He appears to be dressed in dripping wet clothes. He looks at you, smiles and vanishes. Next day you hear that at about the time you apparently saw him, your friend was accidentally drowned.

You will no doubt talk about it as a ghost story. But if you want it to be more than a story, you are bound to look at the events against quite an extensive background, and ask various questions. For example: what is the nature of vision when I can see something with my eyes which is not physically there? This alone involves the whole question of hallucinations and their causes.

If it *was* my friend's spirit, what about his clothes – were they spirit clothes too? Or was he actually transported to my room; or did I see him by some form of telepathy? If the latter, did he create the telepathic vision, or did I? If it was actually my friend, what does *actually* mean, since obviously he was not as I knew him in the body? Or did I imagine the whole thing as a kind of waking dream?

What evidence is there that someone with a distant friend will every so often express his fears for their safety in an anxiety dream? If my friend had already died when he appeared to me, ought I to try from my side to make contact with him again through a seance of some kind? Where is he now?

Before we can begin to think sensibly about questions like these, we need a consistent and reliable background against which to seek an interpretation of happenings like these; happenings which the physical sciences cannot explain.

Let us now begin to set the scene, and show how a Christian is to make a proper judgment.

There are plenty of things in life that anyone can use and enjoy. But there are some things, such as brain surgery, that can only be handled safely by someone who is prepared to go through extensive training. There are a few things, such as heroin injection, that it is both most unwise and most dangerous for anyone to touch at all. Into which category do we place the occult?

If this book simply aimed to establish whether dabbling in the occult is wise or dangerous to humanity, there would be little, once that had been settled, to discuss. Even without acknowledging God, sensible human beings try to do what is wise and avoid what is destructive to individuals and society. So if plunging into the occult is wise, we can all enjoy it if we wish. If it is destructive, neither Christians nor non-Christians ought to touch it.

But for the Christian there are criteria beyond *wise* and *destructive*; namely *right* and *wrong*. Humanists may also use these terms, but while they use them to describe what is expedient or inexpedient, the Christian sees them as related also to God and as eternal realities. He holds that in the person of Jesus Christ, and in the Bible, we have God's revelation of himself and of his relationship with man.

To be in a right relationship with God is to be good (and will result in wisdom, humanly speaking); to be in a wrong relationship with God is to commit sin (and this will result in destructiveness, humanly speaking).

Once we introduce the Bible as God's Word to man, the veil is partly lifted on the unseen and eternal world, since God's purpose is not simply to lay down moral commands, but to unfold the way of union with him. He shows us that we are not the only intelligent inhabitants of this universe, but that there are unseen beings, both on his side and against him.

If experience shows that there are unusual happenings that can be labelled *occult*, a Christian not only looks to see whether they are beneficial or harmful, but tries to interpret them in the light of the total revelation given in Scripture. What then are these experiences?

In this book we shall assume that the Christian revelation, as summarized in the standard Creeds, with its news of God's action in Christ, is so vital that it cannot be abandoned. It is not an option to be believed or discarded. Christianity is not just a matter of doctrine. It has two other aspects: namely personal trust in the Lord Jesus Christ as Saviour, and commitment to him as Lord, borne out by a new way of life.

There is considerable overlapping of moral behaviour between Christians and serious non-Christians. But the claim of Christian doctrine to be a body of revealed truth, and to show in Christ the bridge to God – and therefore the way to goodness – is a claim unique among religions.

2: The Occult

Occult is a blanket word, and we shall need to break it down. Originally, it simply meant *hidden* or *invisible*, but it has obviously come to mean very much more than this. However, its literal use can help to lay a few foundations.

Men and women are part of a visible universe. Whatever views we hold about evolution or its extent, there is no doubt that human beings share many of the bodily functions of the animal world. So much so, that some scientists and psychologists suppose that man and his responses can be understood solely in animal terms.

The Bible uses the term *living creature* both of the non-human animal world (Genesis 1:20,24) and of the human (Genesis 2:7). The identity of the Hebrew words is obscured by the KJV with its translation 'man became a living soul', partially obscured by the RSV and Jerusalem Bible with 'man became a living being', but preserved by the NEB, which has 'living creature' in both places. The point of the other translations is to show that man is more than an animal, but it is best to keep the literal translation. Living creatures are of millions of different varieties. One has to gather from the rest of the Bible what sort of a living creature man is.

The Bible in Genesis 1 makes the point that there was first a creation of the mineral world, then of plants and then of living creatures. Man shares in the mineral and plant world, but *is* a living creature. It is impossible to live in this world unless one has physical substance of some kind. That is why if Jesus Christ was to come to live in this world, he had to receive a physical body.

The Bible, however, indicates that man stands between the visible and an invisible world. There is no doubt that while man is an animal, there is a definite gap between every race of man and the rest of the animals. Man has a plus quality that separates him from them. He can be seen to differ from them genetically, and culturally, and in the mental realm. Only man has ideas, ideals or religions.

As the Genesis story unfolds, it shows that God and man can talk together. Man has animal life but he also has spiritual capacity.

If there are creatures that are purely animal, is it not possible that there are other creatures that are purely spirit? If man shares the one type of life, since he lives in the material world, does he share something of the other type also? The difficulty is that if these other beings exist, they are invisible and undetectable by material instruments, just as God is, and just as the spirit of man is. Then how can we learn about them? Once again we must turn to the Bible as the source book of revelation about the invisible world *so far as it concerns us*.

There are likely to be plenty of points we might wish to know, but we could no more understand them than the dragonfly larva, which lives entirely in the water, could understand the life of the air in which it will one day live. (This analogy is lifted from Mrs Gatty's *Parables from Nature* 1855, one of the finest analogy books ever written, and still in print.)

The Bible clearly confronts us with the sphere of the occult (hidden, invisible), for it emphatically states that God created a realm of spirits without physical bodies. This is not a very fashionable belief today, partly because we do not like to believe in anything that cannot be demonstrated by the physical sciences; partly because the existence of such beings does not necessarily help to explain natural phenomena; and partly perhaps because we have an underlying pride and feel that 'man is the greatest'.

However, the Bible says that such beings actually exist and that they come into a category between God and man. They are referred to as *sons of God* in Job 1:6; 2:1; 38:7, probably in the sense that all are direct creations of God and do not reproduce their kind as animals do (Matthew 22:30). They are also called angels, which refers only to their duties: the Hebrew and Greek words both mean *messengers*.

Some unseen beings are referred to as *spirits*, some as *evil spirits*. Evil spirits are also spoken of as *demons*, which is a transliteration of the Greek plural word *daimonia*. Although the KJV always translates this word as *devils*, the Greek actually uses the word for *devil* (*diabolos*) only in the singular to refer to the supreme spiritual rebel, Satan.

The Bible also speaks of grades of spirit beings. In visions of God in glory, cherubim and seraphim stand by his throne (Isaiah 6:2; Ezekiel 10), and angels (Revelation 4 and 5), and we hear also of Michael the Archangel (Jude 9).

There is mention too of *principalities and powers*; in

Titus 3:1 the term is used of earthly rulers ('rulers and authorities' RSV), but elsewhere they are spiritual rulers, both good (Colossians 1:16) and rebellious (Ephesians 6:12; Colossians 2:15).

Angels are not departed spirits, as spiritualists hold. They existed before man was made (Job 38:4-7). The saved in heaven do not become angels, but are 'like angels' in respect of not bearing children (Matthew 22:30). God uses angels as his messengers, as he uses human beings. They serve those who are being saved (Hebrews 1:14; Acts 12:7).

Angels represent children in heaven (Matthew 18:10). They form the heavenly court (Revelation 5:11). In their duties they are simply the faithful agents of God, responsible to him alone, and may not be worshipped or approached in their own right (Colossians 2:18-23; Revelation 22:8-9). In heaven they are wholly centred in God (Revelation 5:11), but it is impossible to visualise their form of existence which makes them invisible and intangible to us.

There are a number of occasions in the Bible where angels appear in a materialised form. That is to say they were able to take on a temporary physical form so that they could be entertained to a meal by Abraham, pull Lot into the house to escape a hostile crowd, cook a meal for the prophet Elijah, rescue the apostle Peter from prison, and bring the news of the incarnation to the Virgin Mary.

Angels are always sent spontaneously by God and are not first contacted by humans. Christians are forbidden to worship them (Colossians 2:18).

It is puzzling why God should employ angels to do what he could surely do directly himself. And if he uses them, why doesn't he use them more powerfully? It seems that

God delegates duties; he has delegated the spreading of the gospel to mankind, not to angels, since they have no experience of redemption through Christ. The apostle Peter says of the saving work of Christ that it is something into which the angels long to look (1 Peter 1:12).

As well as delegating the spreading of the gospel to mankind, God has also delegated the care of the world to us (Genesis 1:26-30). The world is material and needs the care of physical beings. On the other hand, angels have a spiritual ministry: they are 'ministering spirits sent to serve those who will inherit salvation' (Hebrews 1:14 NIV). We are reminded that some people 'have entertained angels without knowing it' (Hebrews 13:2 NIV).

3: The Unseen World

How far may we experience the ministry of angels today? The daughter of a friend of mine told her mother she was frightened during the wartime bombing of London, until an angel came and sat on her bed. We have the promise of Psalm 91:11: 'He will command his angels concerning you to guard you in all your ways.' We should always live as if this promise is completely effective.

We often hear of miraculous escapes of babies, and it may well be that we are repeatedly delivered from danger through the good hand of angels. I sometimes wonder whether some angels also have duties in the world of nature, but this is speculation.

There are also bad angels who are spoken of as evil spirits or demons. They have a leader, Satan or the Devil, and they are the enemies of God and consequently of humanity. This means that we are not fighting against evil as such, but 'against the rulers, against the authorities, against the powers of this dark world, against the spiritual forces of evil in the heavenly realms' (Ephesians 6:12 NIV).

In the unseen world there are strategists working

against God. Christ 'disarmed the powers and authorities, he made a public spectacle of them, triumphing over them by the cross' (Colossians 2:15 NIV). He won the victory, but the victory still has to be worked out in the name of Jesus Christ the Conqueror.

These spirits were not created evil; like humans they must have fallen. The prophets Isaiah and Ezekiel compare Satan's pride and his desire to be greater than God, in picturing the aims of the rulers of Babylon and Tyre (Isaiah 14; Ezekiel 27). These fallen spirits work against God through men and women, sometimes through demon possession, as we read in the Gospels and Acts, but more often by instilling false ideas into the unconscious or into the suggestion centre reached by hypnotists.

Satan is spoken of by Christ as 'the prince of this world' (John 12:31). The world in this sense is not the good earth, it is the system which is organised as though this life is the whole of existence. Satan would be quite happy with an ideal society – if it could be arranged without God. He even offered to hand over his world system to Jesus Christ, if only he would renounce God and worship Satan himself (Matthew 4:1-10).

So the existence of the Christian church is a continual threat to Satan, and in particular its recognition of Jesus Christ as the one source of salvation. In the early years of the church, Satan seized on people with psychic gifts and turned them into his prophets. This comes out most clearly in 1 John 4:1-3: 'Do not believe every spirit, but test the spirits to see whether they are from God; because many false prophets have gone out into the world' (NIV). The test follows. It is *not* to get an assurance from the trance speaker that he is truly inspired by God. This is how you can recognise the Spirit of God: 'Every spirit that acknowledges that Jesus Christ has come in the flesh is from God, but every spirit that does not acknowledge Jesus is not from God.' The test is a confession of the incarnation of Jesus Christ.

Anything that damages this truth, such as treating Jesus as a God-inspired man, or as having the values of God for us, is an idea promulgated by Satan to divert from Christ as Saviour, Lord and God.

In his attacks on the Christian church, Satan has used two great weapons all down the ages. Both emerge in the book of Revelation, which is best interpreted as the great tribulation of Christians over the centuries, until the final appearance of the Lord from heaven.

The letters to the seven churches of Asia Minor in Revelation 2 and 3 consist of a mixture of warning against false teaching, and encouragement in the face of persecution. The two themes continue through the book, especially in chapter 13 with the persecution and miracle-working beasts. Movements must be tested by what they say about Jesus Christ. Admiration of him is not enough. Miracles and wonders are no proof of truth.

Satan and his spirits can communicate with us to lessen our hold on Christ. In turn, magicians and witches try to communicate with them to draw on their assistance.

So we have good spirits such as angels, and we have bad spirits. The third type of spirit is the departed. There have been spontaneous communications from the departed when a relative has seen, heard or sensed the presence of one who has died. But is it right for us to attempt to communicate with them through mediums? We shall address this question later in the book.

11

Some occultists profess to make use of angels, and profess to contact other beings in between God and man. Thus they speak of *devas* who uphold various aspects of nature such as elves, fairies and undines [water spirits]. If any such spirits exist, they come under the heading of 'the elemental spirits of the universe (Colossians 2:20; Galatians 4:3,9 RSV and NEB).

Christians are warned not to cultivate an interest in them, but rather exhorted to press on in union with the Head of the universe (Ephesians 1:20-23). Why dabble with inferior spirit powers when we can go to the Fountain Head? (Ephesians 3:17-21; Colossians 2:9-10,19).

4: Good and Bad Spirits

If there are both good and bad spirits, this is of considerable importance for our subject. Since the occult apparently involves contact with the spirit world, we need to know what kind of spirits we might encounter. As we have seen in 1 John 4:1-3, Christians are told to test spirit manifestations. We can add 1 Corinthians 12:3: 'Therefore I tell you that no one who is speaking by the Spirit of God says, "Jesus be cursed," and no one can say, "Jesus is Lord," except by the Holy Spirit' (NIV). In other passages we are warned against deception by spirits posing as good, when in reality they are bad (1 Timothy 4:1; 2 Corinthians 11:3-4,14-15; Revelation 12.9).

If occult manifestations come from the spirit world, they must clearly be tested to know whether they are from a good or bad source. But since there are no physical instruments for making such tests, we are dependent on what the Bible says and on what our God-given common sense deduces from the Bible. We want to know all that can be known with reasonable certainty, and we do not want to be deceived.

What then does the Bible say about good and bad spirits? The essence of *good* and *bad* in the Bible is harmony or lack of harmony with God. If we do not understand this, we run into difficulties over how a good God could create bad beings. There will always be a mystery about evil, but essentially evil is saying No to God.

God created, or brought into being, the static mineral world, the growing plant world, and the mobile animal world, each with its own limits. These limits did not include free response at a God-fellowship level. So God created human beings who could say Yes and No consciously and deliberately. An animal enjoys harmony through obeying its drives. Man has harmony by saying Yes to God, through controlling his drives by putting them under the direction of God. He is capable of being God-centred.

The story of the fall in Genesis 3 is the story of a being who once enjoyed harmony and intelligent friendship with God, but who opted out so that he could decide right and wrong for himself. In other words, he became self-centred instead of God-centred. If God had overridden man's free will and kept him as a puppet on a string he could have prevented this; but that would have reduced man to the animal level, and God wanted one who would love him deliberately and willingly. Thus man's first sin was in a sense negative – saying No.

However, from the moment he shifted his control centre from God to himself, man's whole being began to function in a positively bad way. He was like a machine which falls out of alignment at the centre, but which is still connected to its active source of power. The negative lack of alignment then becomes positive damage. So God did not create evil, but he created free beings who were genuinely free to say Yes or No to him, but who in saying No disorganized themselves in a way that made them actively bad.

This is what the Bible says about man, and it makes sense in the light of experience. The Garden of Eden story describes how the first full man and woman made a wrong choice. It shows that *good* is saying Yes to God, and therefore being God-centred, and that *bad* is saying No and taking control into our own hands.

So much for the human side. The Bible goes behind this and shows that the *bad* was already there when man was created. The serpent was a cover for a spirit being who was already evil (Revelation 12:9). Since the good God would not have created a bad being, Satan must have fallen, just as the human race fell. He is not, however, responsible for every sin of man. If he were to be blotted out at this moment, with all his evil associates in the spirit world, human beings would still continue to sin, because they also are rebels in their own right. Christians rightly speak of the three sources of temptation – not one – as 'The world, the flesh and the Devil'.

So we can say that goodness and badness exist in the spirit world. Among human beings also, there is now a twist in all who are born: we refer to it as original sin.

5: Satan and his Works

So far, then, we have seen that human beings are members of a visible and invisible creation. God has shown us in Scripture that there are non-physical and normally invisible beings, some good and some bad, which are like ourselves part of the same creation, and which are like us, personal. When Jesus Christ, with his actual experience of the invisible world, always speaks of Satan as personal, and when he rebukes demons as persons, we cannot suppose that he is teaching that these names simply represent an impersonal force of evil.

Jesus Christ, and the Bible as a whole, speak of one personal Devil given the name Satan (the adversary), always in the singular, and of many demons.

Now, is Satan in any sense the evil counterpart of the God of absolute goodness? He is sometimes popularly imagined as such, but the biblical picture differs from the popular view. Satan is not an eternally existing dark power, corresponding to the eternal light power, the true God. He is a created being who appears as the chief rebel against God. But God declares emphatically that he himself is the sole Absolute. 'I am the first and I am the last; besides me there is no God' (Isaiah 44:6). Thus, Satan is not an absolute god of evil, even though he may assume the place of a god.

The Bible never denies that other beings and things can take the place of God in our devotion, and the second Commandment tells us, 'You shall have no other gods before (or besides) me' (Exodus 20:3). When the Bible speaks in this way of 'other gods', it is admitting their reality in the sense that anything which becomes the object of our worship is to us a god, but it denies that this gives them equality of right with God to be proper objects of worship.

According to Scripture, the primary aim of Satan is to organize a world system from which God is excluded. There is no reason to think he was lying when he told Jesus that all the authority and glory of the world system was his to give to anyone he wished (Luke 4:6). But Jesus refused the gift, which would have meant power without salvation, and chose to go forward to the death on the cross that would cast out 'the ruler of this world' (John 12:31-32), who in spite of all his efforts could not fasten anything on the Saviour (John 14:30).

At the cross, Jesus disarmed Satan and his associates by taking on himself the sins which gave them a hold on the human race (Colossians 2:14-15). Yet Satan still has power to blind human beings to the victory that can free them.

The Bible does not suggest that people are consciously aware of Satan as their god. What Satan is concerned about is that they should not turn to the only true God by way of the cross. Thus he throws a veil of darkness over men's minds (2 Corinthians 4:4) and deceives the whole world

(Revelation 12:9), often making the evil course appear good (2 Corinthians 11:14; Genesis 3:5).

If we can get the picture of Satan as the arch-rebel who uses every possible weapon against God, we shall find it easier to see his hand in the realm of the occult. So long as we think of him as attacking us only through our flesh, we shall miss much of the subtlety of his working. Satan uses the world and the flesh when it suits him, but he employs plenty of other tactics too.

More and more we come to see Satan in the Bible as the twisted arch-humanist. Human humanists are often admirable people. They want to make this world a fit place for human beings to live in, and they want human beings to have freedom to develop as individuals and as members of society. But sadly enough their one condition is that they must do this without God. Thus, they stop us from becoming truly human, since they ban all that Jesus Christ has told us about God.

In Scripture, we mostly see Satan acting against the people of God who know God's distinctive message. He tries to crush Job. He fights to keep Jesus Christ from going to the cross; first by rousing Herod to try to kill him as a baby, then by tempting him in the wilderness to take short cuts to get a following and even to go shares with him in running the world. Later, Satan uses the emotional appeal of Peter to try to turn Jesus' mind from the cross (Matthew 16:21-23). When the cross looms near, he tries to turn all the disciples away so that there will be no one to preach the gospel (Luke 22:31; N.B. the plural 'you').

Satan does not mind the elevated wisdom of the Greeks, since this rejects the cross and the resurrection (1 Corinthians 1:18-25; Acts 17:32). Satan fears the cross. This is not surprising, since on the cross, as we have seen, Christ broke his power.

The victory of the cross has a twofold aspect. Jesus Christ, by bearing the sins of mankind, made it possible for them to escape from the evil, non-God, kingdom of Satan (e.g. Colossians 1:13-20). Also, by doing so, Christ took the headship of the human race that had failed miserably as rulers and directors of the world over which God had appointed them (Genesis 1:26-28).

Jesus Christ was the first Man to live as the perfect Servant of his Father, and although he died voluntarily as if he had been a sinner, his resurrection turned his death into the supreme triumph. (One of the finest summaries of this is Philippians 2:5-11.) Thus he took the right of rule from Satan, the usurper. Christ's people go out in the power of this victory, and the Holy Spirit within them is their living link with him.

Yet God has not exterminated Satan and he still continues the struggle, maybe hoping that he may yet find a way to outwit God. He might try to get his way by killing many of the church and frightening the rest into denying their faith. The New Testament names him as the stirrer-up of persecutions. He is like the lion roaring after its prey (1 Peter 5:8-10). He or his representatives try to force idolatrous submission under threat of death (Revelation 13:11-18).

Yet by the providence of God he has never stamped out any single generation of Christians. In fact, his efforts have given rise to the epigram that the blood of the martyrs is the seed of the church.

We must, however, listen to the warnings of Christ and the New Testament writers that Satan has another line of attack, namely persuading the church to shift from the basic revealed beliefs. Jesus Christ warned of false messiahs and false prophets who would be a menace to the faith of the church (Matthew 24:23-24).

Although Satan is not mentioned here by name, it is clear from the epistles that Satan is in fact the propagator of these attractive anti-Christian ideas. He has his ministers who pose as being on the side of righteousness (2 Corinthians 11:13-15). He can make them appear to be inspired prophets (1 John 4:1-6). He lays traps for Christians, and the property of a trap is that it appears to be normal and good – until it is sprung (1 Timothy 3:7 and 2 Timothy 2:26).

The book of Revelation is intended to throw light on Satan's methods, since he is the deceiver of the whole world (12:9), and the book repeatedly warns against giving way before persecution, or embracing false doctrines (e.g. in the letters to the Churches in chapters 2 and 3).

So-called Satanism is certainly grossly immoral, and Christians are hardly likely to plunge into it. But if we accept the fact that Satan is primarily concerned to divert us into alternatives to the gospel, then we must be prepared for him to offer these alternatives in the form of plausible psychic and spiritual experiences.

For his own reasons, God allows fallen spirits to continue in existence just as he allows fallen man. But wherever God's work of grace and redemption appears, these schemers try to undo it. Since they have had long experience, and their awareness of situations is greater than man's, they are stronger than man.

They can be thrown back only when a Christian clothes himself in the spiritual and moral armour of God (Ephesians 6:10-18) and claims the name and victory of Jesus Christ (Acts 16:18; Ephesians 1:19-23), realizing that already he shares with Christ in his reign (Ephesians 2:6).

So invisible (occult) beings exist, and a whole host of them are active for evil in the universe of which we also are part. Since they regard God as their enemy, and since God is particularly concerned to bring human beings into the maturity of union with himself, they will interfere with his work directly and indirectly whenever they can, and we should expect them both to attack and to use mankind when it suits them.

6: Psychic or Occult?

Although the word *occult* means *hidden*, not everything that is hidden is necessarily occult. The word is not used of every aspect of the hidden unconscious. It is applied to certain strange phenomena that emerge spontaneously, or are produced deliberately from some hidden source. They are strange because they are not subject to the laws of the physical and mental realms by which we consciously live, and which we apply to the understanding of life. *Occult* has a more sinister sound than *psychic*, which in more scientific writing nowadays is often shortened to *psi*, the Greek letter Ψ.

It is often easier to get the feel of word usage than it is to define it closely, but probably one may say that *psychic* speaks of apparent non-physical, yet human, powers that emerge under certain conditions. These would be primarily telepathy, clairvoyance, and precognition (becoming aware of the future). We might include some supernormal healing powers, faculties of water divining, and the ability to see auras of colour or light around the human body. Later we will consider whether it is right to develop these faculties.

The word *occult*, as we have seen, suggests contact with spirit powers, consequent magic and witchcraft. It is impossible to draw a hard line between the two because the occult may include the psychic. If there is contact with spirits, these spirits may use the latent powers of man, and we shall sometimes be faced not only with human beings using their latent human powers, but also with spirits making use of these powers through those who possess them: that is, we shall be faced with *both/and*, as well as *either/or*.

We can illustrate this with the phenomenon of the do-it-yourself occultism of the Ouija board or the inverted tumbler. There was an outbreak of this type of 'communication' in recent years, especially in schools and colleges.

The general principle is that a small group of people rest their fingers lightly on an inverted tumbler, or small board with legs or castors, which is on a smooth table. On the outside of the table there are the letters of the alphabet and numbers, and simple words like *Yes* and *No*. In due course the tumbler or small board spells out answers to questions. The tumbler itself does not give the answers, but the communications come in the name of some spirit who professes to be someone who has passed on.

An earlier form of communication that was popular in the middle of the nineteenth century was table tipping. Here a circle of people rested their hands on a table, often a very solid one, and asked questions of the spirits. They then called through the letters of the alphabet, and the table tilted when the appropriate one was reached. It was a slow process to spell out a sentence in this way!

When one has eliminated deliberate fraud by some member of the group, there is still the possibility of unconscious pushing. This could be eliminated by securely blindfolding everyone who is taking part and then altering the order of the letters.

Sir William Barrett in his book, *On the Threshold of the Unseen* (Kegan Paul, 1918), wrote of some experiments that he and some friends carried out in Dublin with a Ouija board. He describes[*] the complete blindfolding of the group, including himself. Answers were spelled out at high speed, even when the board was turned 180 degrees. Then the letters of the alphabet were shuffled and placed under glass, with the group still wearing blindfolds.

What happened then was that the small board on which the hands were resting 'rushed round and round as if polishing the glass, and then proceeded more slowly to inspect, as it were, each letter of the alphabet, going round each letter till all were located'.

We may stay with Barrett, since the messages he records are typical. Some could be substantiated: names and addresses of people who had recently died and who were unknown to any of the group, were correctly given. There was a remarkable case on the day when the *RMS Lusitania* sank [on the 7th of May 1915]. The group had heard the preliminary report but did not know that a personal friend of theirs, Sir Hugh Lane, was on board. A message was spelled out, 'Pray for the soul of Hugh Lane', and a description followed in the first person of his last minutes before he was drowned. A few minutes later they read the report of the sinking and his name in the evening paper's list of passengers [being sold in the street outside].

Subsequently the alleged Hugh Lane 'wrote' about his will, but failed to explain an important codicil which was

---

[*] Author's original footnote: *Proceedings of S.P.R.*, Vol. XXX, page 243.

disputed! The communicator who claimed to have introduced Hugh Lane to the Ouija board gave his name as Peter Rooney. He told how he had led a life of crime and imprisonment in Boston, and had committed suicide ten days previously by throwing himself under a tram there.

Barrett at once made enquiries from the police in Boston Lincolnshire, and Boston Massachusetts, but no such person as Peter Rooney was known, although several years earlier a Peter Rooney had fallen from the elevated railway in Boston Massachusetts and was laid up for a month. He was still living in Boston.

To turn to a more up-to-date example, the papers got hold of the story of a seance arranged by some of the boys at a Blackpool school. An extract from a taped interview with one of the boys was published in the Inter-School Christian Fellowship periodical *Viewpoint 16* for Autumn 1970. The school was in an area which was the scene of several murders in the past, and the seance was held in a cellar in the school.

The boys used a Ouija board to contact the spirits, and received a communication which claimed to be from a woman who was murdered in 1854 by a man called Mercer. She claimed that an evil presence in the cellar was trying to impede her contact with the group. When she was asked to prove her presence, the temperature of the room began to fall. Although the board told them not to leave the cellar, some of the boys became frightened and the seance broke up.

One further illustration comes from a missionary who, on an evangelistic tour in England, stayed at the home of a Christian lady who had formerly been a spiritualist. He was shown a broken Ouija board on the bedroom shelf, and his hostess told him that she had once used it, but had become more and more suspicious of the origin of the messages that came through. Eventually she asked, 'I am perplexed: what shall I do?' The answer was spelled out, 'Trust and obey, for there's no other way to be happy in Jesus but to trust and obey'.

The words are those of the chorus of a well-known evangelical hymn. However, she pressed further and asked, 'Who are you?' The answer came back, *The Devil*, upon which the leg of the board snapped and it collapsed. It seems strange that the lady kept the board, and this may be one reason why she told the missionary that she was still troubled by evil spirits, even in church during the Communion service.

One hears less today of the planchette. This is similar to the Ouija board, but generally has a pencil as one 'leg', so that it can write or draw.

These then are a few typical occurrences, a crazy mixed bag of obviously true, false and doubtful communications. Is there any single explanation of them, or are we in the realm of multiple agencies? Are they psychic, or are they occult?

7: Spirits or Latent Powers?

We have three possible interpretations of the phenomena that we have taken as an illustration. Firstly, they may be due to the emergence of latent powers in those who are taking part. Or they may be produced by spirits. Or we may combine the two, and say that spirits are able to mobilize the latent powers in man and direct them to their own ends.

The average person jumps straight to the second explanation, and certainly the majority of Christians agree with them that spirits are always responsible, but disagree over the identity of the spirits in question. Nevertheless, I want to argue for the first and third.

Popular belief has always accepted the occurrence of occasional second sight. Until recently no one has seen how to devise the sort of repeatable experiments that a scientist needs if he is to investigate any occurrence. However, many people will have heard of the work initiated by Dr JB Rhine [1895-1980] of Duke University in America. Dr Rhine tested the ability of subjects to discover by telepathy the order of cards in a pack that someone else at a distance was turning up card by card. The cards had five special designs, and it was possible to find whether mathematically the results were above what would be expected by chance. Dr Rhine obtained highly significant results with certain subjects after many runs through the pack.

The most useful book on this subject for the ordinary reader is the well-documented record, *The Mind Readers* (Faber & Faber, 1959) by SG Soal and HT Bowden. The experimenters in this book tested two Welsh country boys of fourteen [Glyn and Ieuan Jones] who had the faculty of telepathic communication. They were tested in front of stage telepathists, who knew all the tricks.

One of their greatest successes was on a cricket field where they sat about eighty feet [24 metres] apart, with a screen between them. They were first thoroughly searched for such things as concealed transmitters. On this occasion, on runs through shuffled packs of twenty-five cards of five different animal pictures, they obtained scores of nineteen, twenty, twenty-three and twenty-five in successive runs; and this was not the only occasion on which they obtained high scores.

Unfortunately, the boys lost their gift in adolescence, and it has now been suggested that they used supersonic dog whistles in their mouths or clothing; but in view of the constant observation and searching they underwent, it is virtually impossible that such a whistle should not have been detected or heard by someone else.[*]

If telepathy or thought reading is a fact, it means that there can be a link-up of minds at a deep level, and that some of the contents of one mind can emerge into the consciousness of another.

It is now impossible to read any serious discussion of spiritualism without encountering the theory of telepathy. The reason why I use the term *spiritualism* in this book is not only for courtesy but because the alternative, *spiritism*, which some Christians prefer, suggests that *all* seance phenomena come directly from spirits. Certainly most mediums assume that they contact the spirits of those who have passed on, and that these spirits then give them messages to relay to someone in the room. But if telepathy is a fact, why should not the medium simply be picking up the picture, voice and message latent in the mind of the recipient?

An important figure in the field of psychical research was Mrs Eileen Garrett [1893-1970], who was looking for an answer to this question for most of her life. In two of her books of autobiography, *My Life as a Search for the Meaning of Mediumship* (Rider, 1939), and *Many Voices* (Allen & Unwin, 1968), she believed that the alleged

---

[*] To test the boys, Soal enlisted the help of Jack Salvin, a professional magician, sceptic, and expert on bogus telepathy, and chair of the Occult Committee of the Magic Circle. Salvin wrote, 'I am completely satisfied, after making all the observations I desired and having permission to do what I wished that no code or trickery took place either on the part of the boys or on the part of anybody else (including the fathers of the two boys); and, in fact, that code or trickery in the experimental conditions I witnessed was impossible.' However, in the 1970s when Soal was too ill to respond, his findings were reportedly declared insupportable by his fellow parapsychologists. This is not to suggest that the boys were or were not frauds, but to show that testing this type of event is extremely difficult.

controlling spirits with their distinctive voices and names were facets of her own personality, and that the communications were built up in picture and voice form from the deep levels of her client's mind. In the second book she even expressed doubt about her own survival after death – which must be unique in a medium!

The telepathy theory is borne out by tests that have been tried from time to time. If an investigator goes to a seance with a fictitious relative or friend in mind, or if he meditates on some character in history or fiction, the medium may reproduce his thoughts in the form of a message from, or description of the person in the client's mind.

In one case a well-known medium at a public meeting picked up a name, Bessie White, who had been invented by one of her clients at a private seance twenty-one months previously. She took up where she had left off, although she had not seen the client between the two meetings, and is unlikely to have recognized her in the large audience.[*]

Investigators who visit various mediums find that if one gets on the wrong tack, others will follow. A relative of mine was told some years ago by three different fortune-tellers that she would die in a car crash at the age of thirty. I am glad to say that she is now past that age. The wrong intuition of the first psychic was picked up as fact by the others.

It is not easy to draw a line between telepathy and clairvoyance, and there is not much point in doing so. Telepathy is the awareness of what is in the mind of someone else, while clairvoyance is the direct perception of

---

[*] Author's original footnote: The case is recorded by KM Goldney in *Proceedings of the Society for Psychical Research*, Vol. XIV, 210-216.

something that nobody is aware of. Both exclude normal perception through the senses.

If I become aware of a picture that you are looking at a hundred miles away, that is assumed to be telepathy. If you place a shuffled pack of cards face downwards on the table, without you or anyone else knowing the order of the cards, and I then write down the order correctly, that is called clairvoyance.

Unfortunately, the distinction is complicated by pre-cognition, or awareness of the future. In extra-sensory perception (ESP) such as telepathy and clairvoyance exhibit, the mind obviously transcends space since it communicates at a distance without any physical means. But it has been found that ESP also transcends time.

Experimentally this has been shown by the ability to get more than a chance average in calling the order of cards as they will be when they are subsequently shuffled. So my supposed clairvoyance may in fact be a telepathic reading of your mind as it will be when you subsequently check the order of the cards! Experimental precognition has confirmed popular belief that some people on occasions can see into the future.

8: Mind Over Matter

We have been considering some psychic capacities inherent in man as an explanation of the knowledge and error communicated by the Ouija board and at the seance. We cannot leave the subject without exploring further reaches of the purely psychic. We must look at what is popularly called the influence of mind over matter.

Perhaps the simplest place to begin is with our own mind and body. It is difficult to define the term *mind*, but we can think of it as our capacity for building on what our physical senses supply. Some would prefer a tighter and more traditional definition, but since there is so much dispute about it among the philosophers we will try to make do with the more general statement.

A word which has emerged in recent times is *psycho-somatic*. Medically this word indicates that it is often not enough to treat the body, since the illness which is perfectly genuine is promoted and kept alive by a disturbed inner attitude. Apart from illness, we all know how there is a constant two-way connection between attitude and bodily well-being, or ill-being. Good news injects a healing psychic force, bad news an unhealthy one. Our mind influences our matter.

If we look away from ourselves, we know that some people radiate an atmosphere of well-being, quite apart from things that they say and do. Many doctors have this additional healing touch. Moreover, there are people who have a natural gift of healing. Often they project healing through the laying-on of their hands.

Some patients who have been helped by such healers as Agnes Sanford [1897-1982] have been aware of a feeling of warmth passing into their body from her hands. Like every natural capacity, this gift should be put into the hands of God to use as he prompts, but only too often it becomes linked to spiritualism.

Since the middle of the nineteenth century, experiments have apparently shown that some people could affect galvanometer needles and electroscopes by an act of will when they extended their hand towards them. Descriptions of these experiments are usefully summarized in Rene Sudre's *Treatise on Parapsychology* (Allen & Unwin, 1960) in the chapter headed *Psychic Fluid*, which is an equivalent name for what I am calling *Psychic Force*.

Yet another name is *Odic* or *Odylic Force*. The word *Od* was coined by the Austrian chemist Dr Karl Reichenbach [1788-1869], in about 1845 to describe what he believed was a natural energy permeating the universe and emanating from a human being as animal magnetism.

In more recent years there have been several experiments conducted to demonstrate or refute the influence of mental concentration on living or material objects. At Duke University for some years Dr JB Rhine [1895-1980] and others claimed that such concentration can affect the fall of dice, whether thrown by hand or mechanically. Thus, willing high numbers has produced a bigger run of high numbers than would be expected by chance.

Others have reported some slight success in willing creatures to move in one direction rather than another, or to one half of a microscope slide rather than the other. Some people claim to have moved small objects under glass. Others are investigating so-called 'green fingers' as influencing the health of plants.

The claims of Uri Geller to bend metal by force of mind are well known, but stage magicians claim that he is no more than a clever conjurer. Perhaps, like some other psychics he has genuine gifts, but helps them out if they fail. He has a British rival in a young man, Matthew Manning [born 1955], who has produced similar results apparently under strict test.

There is the Russian, Nina Kulagina. Detailed reports and films (which I have seen) show that she can move objects even under glass, by drawing her hands over them. Other investigations are well documented in the *Proceedings of the Society for Psychical Research* for January 1976.

One phenomenon is the production of photographs on unexposed films by Ted Serios [1918 – 2006] in America[*]. I am prejudiced against the genuineness of this, since I know

---

[*] Ted Serios was caught faking his images on more than one occasion. He claimed that he could not always perform the feat and, like others, occasionally faked things to put on a good show for paying audiences.

Whether any of the people referred to (including Nina Kulagina) were or are genuine is still a matter for fierce debate, because they have generally been examined by scientists, and not by stage magicians who would be much more aware of fraud and know what tests to set. Some stage magicians claim to be able to replicate all these phenomena, but have not necessarily chosen to do so. An internet search can be informative if done wisely, with arguments for and against, including some YouTube videos.

how spirit photographs have been faked in the past. Spirit photography has gone out of vogue since films replaced plates. Plates could easily be doctored and switched. Films cannot be faked in the same way. But a psychic force that can create light to expose a photograph of an object that is not in the room, opens up yet another area of possibility to bewilder us.[*]

If we admit the realm of psychic force, we can link it to the divining of water and other objects. The water diviner with his hazel twig or other 'instrument' has no conscious awareness of where the water flows, but the presence of the water makes itself felt by an uncontrollable movement of the twig. Since the twig does not move when separated from the diviner, it must be that he supplies the 'current' to a 'radar' twig, and this responds to a field of force that flows from the underground water. It twists when it comes nearest to the water, that is, directly over it.

A gift like water divining has no connection with spir-

---

[*] The use of computer programs like PhotoShop can make changes to photographs and videos that are (almost) impossible to detect, so ghostly figures on the stairs and apparitions at seances are now easier to fake than they have ever been. More recently, photographers with digital cameras have found what seem to be orb-like objects on their photographs taken with flash in dark places. It quickly became a favourite 'proof' of spirits with ghost hunters., but it is now accepted by all but a few that these are caused by dust particles in the air, caught by the flash when particles are floating very close to the lens. The extreme depth of field in small digital cameras allows dust to be recorded as out-of-focus objects, which would be too out of focus to record with film cameras. The flash source being very close to the lens in many digital cameras increases the likelihood of this happening, and the orb shape is the result of the particle being out of focus, combined with the design of the lens aperture. This can happen with rain drops, but being larger, they are easily identified as such. There seem to be no reports of an 'orb' being caught on both images when photographed with stereoscopic cameras, indicating that the object must be very close to the camera, as only one of the pair of lenses is seeing it.

its, and I see no reason why it should not be used for the good of mankind. It is probably an unusual but natural sensitivity to radiations.*

Although diviners have sometimes failed completely under test, they have a sufficient run of success to make it worth the while of big companies to use them to discover water.

In discussing telepathy we concluded that mind can be in contact with mind at a deep level. Can this contact ever be used actively so that one mind exerts an influence on another? Witchcraft and magic, which we examine later, work on the assumption that it can. They attempt to mobilize psychic force, although they often combine this with the invocation of supernatural beings. Witchcraft in one form or another has been practised down the ages. Certain men and women have inherited or developed powers of working spells.

---

* Divining for treasure on a map using a pendulum or crystals cannot use the same natural sensitivities to the ground as divining for water when out in the field with rods. It is probably important to understand this difference, before condemning all divining as being influenced by spirits. The word 'dowsing' may be more helpful when applied to searching for water flowing underfoot, removing any suggestion of divine or spirit intervention.

9: Some Questions

We have reached a line of division. Some would be happy to stop with the hypothesis that psychic force is an explanation of all occult phenomena. On the other hand, a number of Christians remain convinced that evil spirits are at the bottom of everything. Here let me say that even if natural psychism alone could be the explanation, it would not follow that all use of psychic gifts is harmless. We shall take up some reasons for this later, but meanwhile from the purely practical point of view it is worth reading the cases that Kurt Koch presents in his book, *Between Christ and Satan* (Evangelization Publishers, 1961).

Dr Koch [1913-1987] was a German evangelical pastor with a special mission to people who had been inwardly and outwardly attacked as a result of participating in occult practices. In many of his quoted cases the attacks came after such apparently simple things as fortune-telling and reciting charms, as well as after direct involvement in trying to contact spirits.

However, we are now looking for evidence for direct spirit intervention, although we shall not rule out the likelihood that spirits can use the natural psychic forces already in man. Let us turn first to the Bible.

A Christian is bound to give serious consideration to what the Bible says about our communication with the spirit world, and one cannot deny that the Bible is emphatically against attempting it. Unfortunately the KJV is not as clear as it might be, and by its regular use of the term *familiar spirits* it switches our mind away from mediumship to witchcraft.

What are familiar spirits? The first known occurrence of this term in English literature is in the Geneva Bible of 1560, a translation made by exiled Protestants during Queen Mary's reign. During the second half of that century there are many references to familiars as the demons in the form of animals that were given to a witch when she made a pact with the Devil. *Familiar* comes from the Latin, and means *servant*.

The familiar served the witch in magical spells, and then was rewarded by sucking blood from some spot on the witch's body. This account of familiars is almost entirely English and Scottish. They are not mentioned in Elizabeth's Statute against witchcraft in 1563, but the James I Statute of 1604 refers to any person who shall 'entertain, employ, feed, or reward any evil and wicked spirit to or for any intent or purpose'.

Evidence of the existence of these familiars was obtained by similar brutal psychological and physical methods to those that have been used to extract political confessions in modern times. This worthless evidence was supplemented by the discovery of any wart or mole or other blemish on the body of the witch, since this mark would be regarded as the teat from which the familiar was fed.

The KJV translators, thinking only of their current

witch trials, augmented the Geneva references to familiar spirits. In Leviticus 19:31 we read, 'Regard not them that have familiar spirits, neither seek after wizards, to be defiled by them: I am the LORD your God' (KJV). The result of this translation was that, as Dr Basil Atkinson says in his Commentary,

'The mediaeval and early post-Reformation world completely misunderstood the meaning of the witchcraft referred to in the Bible ... Not till the return of spiritism and mediumship in the 19th century did the world know experimentally the witchcraft of the Bible'.

There are several references to occult practices in the first five books of the Bible, but the fullest is in Deuteronomy 18:9-14, which lists people whose practices are banned. After a denunciation of human sacrifice, there follow three groups: fortune-tellers; those who attempt to cast spells and work magic; and finally those who claim to make contact with the departed. The RSV translates these as 'a medium, or a wizard, or a necromancer' ['a medium or spiritist or who consults the dead' (NIV)].

The first practitioner is one who consults an *obh*. The second is *yiddeoni,* from the Hebrew root *yadah,* meaning *to know*; hence a knowing one. Is this a man, or as the lexicon says, a familiar spirit who is believed to have superior knowledge? The idea still lingers that the departed speak with some special authority. The third practitioner is one who inquires of the dead, which is the literal translation. This should in fact not be translated in the RSV as *necromancer,* which commonly suggests the use of a corpse for magical purposes. *Dead* here is the equivalent of our *departed*.

Let us take the middle word and note its use in Scripture. It is coupled with *obh* again in Leviticus 19:31: 'Do not go after the *obhoth* and the *yiddeonim*'. In Leviticus 20:27 the death penalty is prescribed for a man or woman in whom, or with whom, is an *obh* or a *yiddeoni*.

So it is reasonable to argue that an *obh* and a *yiddeoni* are very similar. The book of Leviticus suggests that both are sought by a client via the person who possesses them. This is still clearer in Isaiah 8:19: 'When they say to you, Consult the *obhoth* and the *yiddeonim* who chirp and mutter, should not a people consult their God? Should they consult the dead on behalf of the living?' Consulting the *obhoth* and the *yiddeonim* is paralleled with consulting the departed.

Isaiah mentions the change of voice which characterises some communications via mediums today. He speaks of it varying between the twitter of a swallow and the low pitch of the dove (29:4 literal Hebrew).

Another famous biblical incident concerns the woman of Endor, whom King Saul consulted in an effort to communicate with the departed spirit of the prophet Samuel. She was not a witch, as she is often called, but was certainly a medium who was expected to contact the departed. She is twice called, literally, 'a woman who is mistress of an *obh*' (1 Samuel 28:7).[*] The word translated *mistress* is the feminine of *baal* (lord or owner), and it

---

[*] Interestingly, the fourteenth century Wycliffe translation from the Latin, before the English obsession with witches, has, 'Seek ye to me a woman having a fiend speaking in the womb ...' which seems to express the situation well.

would make good sense if the woman spoke of 'my control'. It is true that she is taken over by the spirit, but the spirit is dependent upon her ownership if it is to manifest itself.

Commentators differ over the question of whether the spirit of Samuel was actually materialised by the medium at Endor. I believe that this was an exceptional situation which surprised the medium herself. She saw 'a god coming up out of the earth' (1 Samuel 28:13 RSV). Evidently she left while Samuel was speaking to King Saul, since afterwards 'she came to Saul', an act which a medium would not do if she was supporting a materialised spirit.

Unlike alleged spirits today who appear to be glad to communicate, Samuel asks why he has been disturbed. Later in the Bible we are told that Saul died for his unfaithfulness to God, in disobeying the commandment not to consult mediums (1 Chronicles 10:13).

From all this evidence we may fairly conclude that the mediums mentioned had contact with, or were possessed by, spirits. If we are to draw a distinction, we might argue from modern mediumship that the *obh* is the regular control, and the *yiddeonim* are other spirits who can be called up, and who respond in voices which are different from that of the medium.

10: Warnings

Despite the Old Testament ban, some Christians believe there is a place for Christian mediums (or sensitives) today. They quote some of the minor commands of the Old Testament Law, and say that since they have been set aside we need not retain the ban on mediumship. However, there is a distinct difference between the food laws, which were repealed by Christ, and laws which have to do with permanent spiritual relationships. Moreover, such an argument would allow Christians to use sorcery, magic and divination, which are here put alongside mediumship.

There is an extraordinary book called *Spiritualism in the Old Testament* by Canon Maurice Elliott (Psychic Book Club, 1940). In it he describes almost every phenomenon in the Old Testament in terms of spiritualism. He claims that Yahweh, or Jehovah, is the spirit guide of Israel, but is not God himself. The words 'God spake' are, he claims, 'an offence to the intelligence'. Moses is 'that grand old medium'. The answer to this strange idea is what Jesus

Christ himself said of *Yahweh,* quoting from the Old Testament: 'Worship the Lord your God' (Matthew 4:10), and the original Hebrew in Deuteronomy 6:13 shows that 'the Lord' is *Yahweh.*

Obviously we must look at the light the New Testament throws on any possible lifting of the ban. The spirit in the mediumistic girl at Philippi, who hindered the work of the apostle Paul, was treated as an enemy to be cast out, despite the fact that it witnessed to the truth of the Christian gospel (Acts 16:16-18). But more importantly, when the apostle Paul comforts Christians for the loss of loved ones he does not say, as spiritualists would, 'Next Sunday our prophet-medium will put you in touch with them.' Instead, he assures them that in Christ, who has risen from the dead, they will meet their loved ones again.

The ban on direct communication with spirits has not been lifted. The Old Testament speaks of false prophets, and the New Testament does the same. The spirits have to be tested to discover their attitude to Jesus Christ's incarnation and Deity (1 John 4:1-3). The test is not concerned with establishing whether the communicating spirit is or is not your pious grandfather, for the New Testament knows of no such mediumistic communication from anyone who has passed on.

Is it possible to discover any reason for the ban on mediumship? A committee set up by the Archbishop of Canterbury many years ago gave a qualified assent to some spiritualist claims, but pointed to the lack of evidence that spiritualist contacts assisted spiritual growth. We might add that they can actually hinder the truth of the Christian gospel. Lord Dowding [1882-1970, of RAF wartime Fighter Command fame], a staunch spiritualist, wrote:

The first thing which the orthodox Christian has to face is that the doctrine of the Trinity seems to have no adherents in advanced circles of the spirit world. The Divinity of Christ, as a co-equal partner with the Father, is universally denied. Jesus Christ was indeed the Son of God, as also are we sons of God ... We[*] are taught to believe in the remission of sins to the penitent, through the virtue of Christ's sacrifice and atonement. This doctrine, Imperator vigorously combats in a score of places.
[*Many Mansions*, Rider, 1943]

This is borne out in a book written many years ago by the Revd Stainton Moses, *Spirit Teachings* [1883]. In it he describes how he was led step by step from the truths he accepted at his ordination.

It is not true that every medium and every person who attends a spiritualist service disbelieves the Christian faith. There are several spiritualist groups with different sets of beliefs about Jesus Christ. But those who go deeply into spiritualism almost inevitably find themselves caught up in alien philosophy.

We have seen how evil spirits attack the Christian faith by speaking through false prophets, and one can well believe that the inspiration of some messages from beyond come from this source. Spiritualist papers frequently carry warnings against contacts with evil spirits, and established mediums teach beginners how to distinguish true communicators from false. Possibly their instructions do

---

[*] Author's original notes: 'We are taught' – that is, orthodox Christians are taught. Imperator is the pseudonym of one of these advanced spirits.

not go far enough.

This does not necessarily mean that when a widow or widower consults a medium, the departed husband or wife is impersonated by an evil spirit. Most mediums claim to have the gift of clairvoyance, and in good faith they may draw the memories and description of the person who has passed on from the person who wants a message, although the memories are perceived as actually coming from the departed.

We have already referred to Mrs Eileen Garrett [1893-1970], one of the most respected mediums of recent times. She came to believe that this was the explanation of her gift. In her autobiography [*My Life*, Psychic Book Club, London, 1939], she writes:

I have become aware that I draw the knowledge which helps me build the images of the dead relatives and friends of those who need help from the subconscious minds of the sitters.

She may well be right, and while the seeker receives comfort and reassurance, this does not come directly from the departed but from his or her own loving memories.

In these days when extravagant claims are frequently made about possession by evil spirits, it is remarkable that the experienced exorcist, Dom Robert Petitpierre [who died 20 December 1982], says that he had come across only one case of a person taken over by a demonic force. He recognises physical and psychological causes for some inner troubles, and also puts down poltergeist phenomena to psychic disturbances and general ESP capacities. His exorcisms are chiefly concerned with what he calls 'little devils'; that is, spirits who disturb people and places.

Such ideas have made me think again about the existence of earthbound spirits, tied to some place or object on earth, and who now cannot detach themselves from it. Both Dom Robert and another Christian writer, John Richards, quote Christ's words about laying up treasure in heaven, and not on earth, 'for where your treasure is, there will your heart be also.' Thus a person may remain mentally bound to his treasure after death.

Both the authors mentioned write about the imprinting of places by emotional events which have occurred in the past. This certainly explains hauntings where people see or hear past events as a kind of video. Some of these earthbound appearances may well be imprints of this nature. Footsteps on the stairs, or an old man in the doorway, may be earthbound relics rather than earthbound human spirits, and people psychically tuned may pick them up.

The cases quoted by Dom Robert certainly respond to actual prayer and the celebration of Holy Communion. On the other hand, Dom Robert also tells of the exorcism of accident black-spots where accidents occur through motorists swerving to avoid a non-existent person in the road. The place itself can be exorcised, but he does not believe that the spirit of someone killed there actually returns on each occasion. Rather, he accepts that the accident has been 'imprinted'.

Although I am reluctant to accept the idea of earthbound human spirits, I cannot find anything in the Bible to forbid such a belief. But if exorcism is the driving out of evil spirits, I would not command any spirit who might conceivably be earthbound to go to the place prepared for the Devil and his angels, but rather to go to the place that God had prepared for it. It might not be a 'lost' soul, for even a Christian may be over-devoted to his or her possessions!

As we have seen, some Christians believe there is a place for mediums today. It is important to distinguish between mediums who are psychically sensitive, and those who go further and appear to make contact with the actual world of spirits. A sensitive may clairvoyantly sense the memories of people so that they seem to be seeing or hearing the people who exist in memory. A sensitive can also pick up the feeling of a place where, say, some tragedy has happened, or where some person has lived under emotional stress. They may then see this person as a video ghost.

There is a definite borderline between the psychic and the occult, but it is easy to step over it inadvertently. The danger may come when a psychic approaches spiritualists in order to improve his or her gift. The realm of psychic ability is neutral, and it may be used for the self, for God, or for Satan.

Do-it-yourself means of communication with the spirit world include the Ouija board, the sliding tumbler and the now rarer planchette. Again and again, people who have taken part in such activities have suffered as a result, seeming to be haunted by some evil presence. I have heard a number of reports of the tumbler exploding when certain questions were asked.

A Christian girl, who had been in the room during a session, came to see me. Though she had not taken part in the seance, she had the unpleasant experience of the tumbler flying off the table and hitting her in the stomach, leaving what looked like a burn on her skin. It is remarkable that Christians and spiritualists are both agreed about the danger of contacting an evil spirit by this means.

Having shown that a communication may actually be clairvoyance from the medium, a drawing out of the medium's own subconscious ideas or feelings, or an impersonation by a false spirit – are any messages in fact genuine? Some members of the Society for Psychical Research, with all the evidence that the society has amassed [since 1882], are not convinced that any messages are genuinely from the departed.

Even if we conclude that some communications *are* genuine, are they of any value? Many of them are simply concerned with proving survival, as for example in the so-called cross-correspondences in which abstruse crossword type clues, given to several mediums, are brought together to make sense. Others describe experiences much as they were on earth, or as with messages from FWH Myers (1843–1901) that we will come to later, continue ideas they had while in the body. It would appear that they have somehow missed the New Testament promises, 'That you may also be where I (Christ) am' (John 14:3); 'Depart and be with Christ' (Philippians 1:23). None of this comes through in their messages. The opinions of the spirits are of no greater value than those they held on earth.

When all is said and done, the Bible bans deliberate contacts with the spirit world other than with God. If contacts were impossible, it would hardly have banned them. In our 'liberated' society there are certain activities which people indulge in simply because they are available. They are not, for this reason, advisable or right. Drugs may break through the barrier of consciousness, but they damage the personality. Smoking eases tension, but may kill the body. So God, who knows, warns against satisfying our curiosity by consulting spirits.

The Bible sets its face against all forms of magic and the occult. It is consequently in striking contrast to almost every religion and society in the world, where from the very earliest recorded time until the present day, superstition and magic have been treated as legitimate for those who know how to use them.

In general, the biblical attitude is entirely consistent in its basic background, namely the supremacy of the One God, a jealous God who has made men and women for himself. His jealousy is desire for their welfare. He has given them a material world in which to develop, but they have an awareness under the surface that life is more than material.

The hunger of the heart is meant to find satisfaction in God, but it is possible to pull aside the blanket of the dark and penetrate a sphere of non-material forces and experiences. One may even break into a world of entities that are as enticing as God, without making demands for moral and spiritual obedience. Somehow, non-material powers – personal or impersonal – assume the status of a capricious god.

Magic goes further. Either by his own inner resources or by collusion with spirit entities, or both, the practitioner attains mysterious power that is not open to the average person, although the practitioner can distribute the benefits or curses to his clients and their enemies. The magician eats of the tree of the knowledge of good and evil, and becomes as God.

The consistent attitude of the Bible is that while there

are non-material and spiritual levels, it is for God to use them as he sees fit: it is not for man to intrude into their domain. The Bible, claiming to speak as the revelation of God, and knowing man's weakness for substitute religious experiences, bans those avenues into the occult that at the very least are blind alleys that obscure the way to God, and at worst are roads to destruction.

For reference:
Eileen Garrett: *My Life as a Search for the Meaning of Mediumship* (Rider, 1939). Also, *Many Voices* (Allen & Unwin, 1969)
Dom Robert Petitpierre: *Exorcising Devils* (Hale, 1976)
John Richards: *But Deliver us from Evil* (Darton, Longman &Todd, 1974)

11: Spirit and Mind Together

Many Christians may think I am almost blasphemous when I say that I believe Jesus made use of the psychic. If I am right that the psychic is within the human dimension, then Jesus Christ as perfect man must have shared in it. We have become confused in thinking that all of his unusual actions are a proof of his Deity. Certainly they were a proof of his *Messiahship* – but that is not the same thing.

There is nothing wrong in the idea of Jesus as a perfect human healer. Modern healers and their patients are often aware of some force or energy passing from one person to another, much as Jesus felt when the woman touched him in the crowd (Mark 5:25-30). We are not belittling the power of God if Jesus put his human psychic faculties entirely under his Father's control.

The same may be true of Jesus' faculty of clairvoyance when he 'saw' Nathanael sitting alone under a fig tree, presumably meditating on Jacob's vision at Bethel (John 1:47-51; Genesis 28:12). Jesus' talk with the woman at the well at Samaria showed a knowledge of her which could similarly have come through clairvoyant perception (John

51

4:16-29).

When we come to the miracles of creativity, we clearly go beyond the purely human. There is the turning of water into wine by Jesus at the marriage feast at Cana (John 2:1-11), and the repeated multiplication of the loaves and fishes (Matthew 14:13-21; 15:32-38).

These stories reflect two interesting facts. First, Jesus did for others what he refused to do for himself when he would not turn stones into bread during his temptation in the wilderness (Matthew 4:2-4). Secondly, there is no miracle in the Bible that involves creation out of nothing. Water was turned into wine, of which it constitutes the greater part. The loaves and fishes were multiplied from those which were offered by the young boy.

As further examples of Christ's power to restore, we notice his recall of people from the dead, such as the daughter of Jairus (Mark 5:35-43), and the widow's son at Nain (Luke 7:11-16). It may be argued by some that these were restored so soon after death that they had merely been in trance. But the raising of Jesus' friend Lazarus, after four days in the grave, is in a completely different category (John 11:17-44).

Some readers may argue that the prophet Elisha was similarly used to multiply food (2 Kings 4:42-44), and also to raise a child who was said to have died (2 Kings 4:18-37); and that Elijah was used in a similar way to maintain a constant supply of flour and oil in a widow's house, and to bring her son to life again (1 Kings 17:8-24).

Certainly there are similarities between these and the miracles of Jesus Christ. But the difference is in the approach. Whereas the prophets do not give the impression of 'doing' the miracles, by contrast Jesus himself is the doer.

It seems likely that Balaam, whose story is told in the book of Numbers, was primarily a clairvoyant who used his gift for money. He had some contact with God, although he did his best to evade what he knew to be God's command.

Balaam did not at first see the angel who stood in his way, although he read the braying of his ass clairvoyantly (Numbers 22:21-35). When he did see the angel, it was the Lord who opened his eyes. It is true that in trance Balaam received and spoke the message of God (Numbers 24:3-4), but his own heart was untouched. He had his revenge on God for making him bless Israel, by becoming an authority figure who lured the people into throwing themselves into religious prostitution with the Baal of Peor (Numbers 25:3; 31:16). In the New Testament Balaam is cited as an example of evil (2 Peter 2:15; Jude 11).

No doubt Balaam had a clairvoyant revelation to produce in support of his advice, but his life shows how clairvoyant gifts can be misused.

Psychic capacities should not be cultivated and developed. I have often found that Christians are relieved to be told that spontaneous experiences of clairvoyance, precognition and ghosts are not of the Devil. Their 'gifts' are to be put to God's service, to be used or taken away by him. Attempts to cultivate them can easily lead to a wrong or selfish use. If they are accepted as they are, God will make use of them when he needs them.

There is a striking story in the book of Kings which fifty years ago was frequently ridiculed. An iron axe-head fell into the River Jordan. The young prophet who dropped it was worried because it was borrowed, and he couldn't afford to replace it. He appealed to Elisha who threw a stick into the water, whereupon the iron came to the surface and the young man retrieved it (2 Kings 6:1-7).

Today we may look for demonstrations of the power of mind over matter. I think we can keep an open mind about the role of spirits in table-lifting and poltergeist activity. If they are behind the phenomena they do not generate the psychic power themselves, but seize on what emerges from the sitters at the seance, or the person under stress.

We still know very little about psychic or mind forces, although they certainly exist. If spirits can use them, then God can use them yet more fully. Returning to the story of the floating axe-head, it is not irreverent to see God guiding Elisha and drawing out of him the necessary psychic power to lift the iron.

In this chapter we have concentrated on the ability of mind to influence other minds and material objects. We must remember that spirit and mind may work together so that spirit may influence mind. When God the Holy Spirit dwells within the human spirit, he uses the mental and physical abilities which make up a total human being.

I have written of the psychic faculty as a neutral gift, so I ought to answer the question of whether we should seek to develop it, as we develop other gifts which God has given to us. I have suggested that the gift may be put into the hands of God to use; or it may gravitate into the demonic occult; or be used for self.

Experience shows that attempts to develop the gifts tend to draw a person away from God, and to minister pride in the possession of something which others do not possess. Some have developed the power to influence others by psychic means. Also, the borderline between psychic and occult is thin, and a gift of clairvoyance and clairaudience may lead to a mediumship which is contact with spirits.

There is a warning in the life of the famous Edgar Cayce [usually pronounced Casey. 1877-1945], who was a strong evangelical Christian in the USA, and who had the extraordinary psychic gift of diagnosing and prescribing for illnesses when he was under trance. There was no question of spiritualism. Then one day he came under the influence of a man who held theosophical views, and under trance Cayce began to give back strange theosophical ideas, including astonishing revelations about reincarnations of Jesus Christ. It is only too easy for psychic gifts to go astray. The false prophets were psychic, but they were false.

If one has unusual psychic gifts, they should be deliberately put into God's hands to use as he sees fit. He may use them only occasionally, but he *must* take the initiative. Thus God may use the influence of intense prayer that he inspires; but alternatively we may generate an influence and direct it to accomplish something that we believe is right, but we may be wrong.

12: Encounters with God

Sceptics believe that any encounter with God is more than unusual – it is impossible, since there is no God! Even for the Christian such an event is truly mysterious. Nevertheless, the Bible records a number of appearances of God to man.

We immediately recall what John says. 'No one has ever seen God' (John 1:18), a sentence repeated in his first letter (1 John 4:12). Does this contradict the alleged appearances of God to Abraham, Moses, Isaiah and others?

It has always seemed to me that the more obvious a contradiction appears in the Bible, the less likely it is to be a true contradiction. The apostle John knew the Old Testament records perfectly well. In addition, his own Gospel tells us that Christ, the Word, was God (John 1:1), and that in his hearing Jesus Christ had accepted the confession of Thomas of him as God (John 20:28).

So the writer, John, himself had seen God – although he says that no one has ever seen God! Perhaps John gives us a clue in John 1:18; where he continues, 'The only Son[*] who is at the Father's side, has made him known', and again records the words of Jesus, 'Anyone who has seen me has seen the Father' (John 14:9).

Jesus and John are evidently referring to physical sight. Moreover, when John writes of 'seeing God', he clearly means God in his essential being. Some scholars point out that in the Greek original of John 1:18 and 1 John 4:12 the word 'God' does not have a definite article in front, and might well be translated 'Deity'. However, this is not conclusive, since John sometimes uses the word with the article and sometimes without. Yet we may still hold that the underlying meaning is 'Deity'.

A comparison might be drawn with electricity. No one has ever seen electricity, although we have all seen it in action as light and heat. Similarly, although God in his absolute essence remains invisible to us, he may show himself in a form that can be perceived.

How, then, does God show himself? Christians may be aware of his presence, although we do not create his presence with us. Christians vary in their perception of him. Some have a strong awareness of God's presence with them. Others are aware of his presence in them through his Holy Spirit. Still others are aware of his presence above them, especially when they come before him in prayer. These three experiences are not mutually exclusive, but most of us are conscious of one more than another.

If we change *see* for *perceive*, we can say that these are ways in which we 'see' God, although not with our eyes. There is nothing unusual here.

---

[*] Author's original footnote: Some ancient manuscripts even say 'the only God'.

We enter the realm of the unusual when we come to visions of God. The word 'vision' is derived from the Latin word 'to see', so a vision of God is a seeing of God.

Whereas physical sight can be shared, a vision is essentially private, even if more than one person shares it, as happens very occasionally. In this way it has some similarity with a dream, and indeed the Bible occasionally links dreams and visions, for example when a dream is called 'a vision in the night' (Isaiah 29:7), and Daniel has 'a dream, and visions passed through his mind' (Daniel 7:1 NIV).

A dream has the same quality of sight as has a vision. Even if I am sleeping in a dormitory, no one in the room sees what I see in my dream, and yet afterwards I can tell them what I saw. When Isaiah went into the temple and 'saw the LORD seated on a throne' (Isaiah 6:1), it is extremely doubtful whether any of the other worshippers saw the Lord.

It is unlikely that any others beside Amos saw the Lord standing by the idolatrous altar (Amos 9:1). This distinction is clearly made in Daniel 10:7. 'I, Daniel, was the only one who saw the vision; the men with me did not see it, but such terror overwhelmed them that they fled and hid themselves' (NIV). They felt an acute sense of God's presence, but saw nothing.

How can anyone see what is not there for others to see? (Notice I don't say 'what is not there at all'.) The nature of sight and hearing is a mystery; all that we know is that electrical impulses travel to the brain, and the appropriate parts of the brain transform the impulses into pictures or meaningful sound. If these parts of the brain are stimulated directly, the person will 'see' the appropriate picture or 'hear' a voice. This can be done by hypnotism, and as we will see later, a person can be induced to see a named person enter the room and sit down on a chair which is actually empty.

The person concerned is seeing what is totally unreal, and his or her vision is like the hallucinations of someone who is mentally disturbed. Those who are interested in such experiences distinguish between hallucinations without any underlying reality, and veridical (truth-conveying) hallucinations which correspond to something real.

There are many examples of someone at the point of death appearing to a friend at a distance. And so we return to the start of the very first chapter of this book, the vision of the distant friend in dripping clothes, which would suggest drowning. If news comes next day that this friend was drowned at the time of the vision, then that is a veridical hallucination.

I am making no more than a tentative suggestion about how God made himself seen in visions. All we can do is to indicate that a vision accords with human experience. But how can we know whether the visions of God recorded in the Bible are veridical, or wholly hallucinatory? After all, the false prophets spoke 'visions from their own minds' (Jeremiah 23:16); that is, their visions were self-suggested and purely hallucinatory.

Often we have to solve this sort of problem by commonsense. For example, was Jesus Christ hallucinating when he claimed to be the Messiah? Were the disciples hallucinating when they claimed to have seen Jesus alive after he had been buried? In other words, does the Christian faith rest upon hallucination?

Commonsense tells us that the total record of the Bible forms a consistent and veridical pattern, like all the pieces of a jigsaw coming together, leading to Christ, although many authors were involved in writing it. Moreover, Christian experience from the beginning to the present-day leads us to accept Christ's awareness of himself, and the assertion of the resurrection, as God's truth.

In the Old Testament the various visions seen by the prophets can be tested by their consistency with the total plan of God. God chose different interpreters who could most easily grasp the various angles of truth. These angles may differ, but the central core is the same, so that one prophet or writer does not contradict another.

The prophet Jeremiah sums it up when he says of the false prophets, 'If they had stood in my council (says the Lord) ... they would have turned (my people) from their evil ways' (Jeremiah 23:22). This was the consistent mark of all the true prophets.

13: Seeing God

We must say something more about the vision of God that Ezekiel describes in his first chapter, since this vision has suffered by being taken as the actual appearance of a UFO, when writer seems to have unthinkingly copied writer. If only they had looked at their Bible! We are told that UFOs come in all shapes and sizes, but I have never heard of one propelled by creatures with heads like a lion, an ox, an eagle and a man, and driven by a man sitting on top!

The form of the man carried on the throne is clearly God as seen in vision, a fact which emerges even more clearly in the reappearance of the vision when God departs from the temple (Ezekiel chapters 9 and 10), and in its reappearance in the prophet Ezekiel's symbolic temple (43:1-4).

In Daniel 7:9-14, Daniel has a vision of God, the 'Ancient of Days', seated on a throne in heaven. The setting of this vision is more or less repeated in the revelation that John was given (Revelation 4 and 5). There is in addition the vision of God which Micaiah was shown (1 Kings

22:19), where again the Lord is seated on his throne. Then there is Jeremiah's vision of the Lord's hand touching his mouth (Jeremiah 1:9). One wonders whether ordinary worshippers occasionally had a vision of God when they came to the tabernacle or the temple, as Isaiah did.

An interesting verse is found in Psalm 84:7 where translators are divided over the best rendering of the Hebrew. The traditional translation is, 'each appears before God in Zion' (KJV). Some modern versions prefer 'the God of gods will be seen in Zion' (NEB, GOOD NEWS BIBLE). There is no reason why the second should not describe a genuine vision (so also Psalm 63:2, but not, as some modern interpreters have held, the sight of some image of Yahweh in the temple (Exodus 20:4).

Although God apparently showed himself in visionary human form, he also appeared in a more 'general' form. He was perceived as overwhelming glory in a bright cloud. At the dedication of the temple, the glory of the Lord entered as a cloud, so bright that the priests could not stay to minister (1 King 8:10-11).

When the people came out of Egypt 'the LORD went ahead of them in a pillar of cloud … and by night in a pillar of fire …' (Exodus 13:21). Later, the cloud covered the tabernacle and remained while the people stayed in any place, but rose and guided them when the time came to move on (Exodus 40:34-38).

On Mount Sinai the Lord showed his presence in thunder, fire and cloud (Exodus 19:16-20), and spoke to Moses in the cloud on the mountain (Exodus 20:21-22; 24:18). Although the cloud on the mountain appeared to be dark, the Lord's presence was so bright that Moses' face carried the reflected radiance for days (34:29-35).

It would seem that the people saw the signs of God's presence in these phenomena, while Moses actually saw God. When God communicated with Moses, 'with him I speak face to face, clearly, and not in riddles; he sees the form of the LORD' (Numbers 12:8).

Somehow it is not too difficult to accept a vision that is perceived by the inner eye. It is much more difficult and very unusual to be faced with the experience of a spiritual being in the realm of the material. Yet the Bible describes physical appearances of God and of angels.

Such appearances of God are very rare. We think of the appearance of God accompanied by two angels to Abraham in his old age, as told in Genesis 18 and 19. Here Abraham sees three men standing at his tent door, and invites them to a substantial meal. They seem to be ordinary travellers until one of them, who is said to be the Lord [Jehovah], promises that Sarah will have a son in the spring.

After this, the Lord tells Abraham that he is about to destroy the cities of Sodom and Gomorrah. 'Abraham remained standing before the LORD' and prayed for the city to be spared if there were at least ten righteous people in it. Then 'the LORD left' and 'the two angels arrived at Sodom in the evening'. The story is consistent all the way through. God appeared in a form that could eat and drink. He is not a ghost, nor is he a subjective vision.

There is a yet more astonishing appearance of God at the ford of the River Jabbok (Genesis 32:22-32). 'A man wrestled with Jacob until the break of day', and although in the morning the man refused to tell Jacob his name, Jacob said, 'I saw God face to face, and yet my life was spared.'

So we are faced with two incidents that are totally outside our experience, and indeed beyond our imagination. Some spiritualists find an easy solution. Maurice Elliott (*Spiritualism in the Old Testament*, Psychic Book Club, 1940) writes, 'Abraham must have been a powerful materializing medium, for the three visitants were fully materialized'.

He must indeed have been powerful if he could materialize God, let alone two others at the same time! Elliott, as we saw earlier, regards Yahweh as a great spirit guide, in spite of the fact that Jesus Christ believed in him as God, and taught us to worship him.

There are also cases in the Bible of a mysterious figure described as '*the* angel of the Lord', and not simply *an* angel. The strange thing about this figure is that he is spoken of as the angel, but speaks as the Lord. It may be that we are to regard him as the Lord's ambassador. However, many scholars, including myself, believe him to be the Second Person of the Trinity, and so the Lord himself.

This 'angel' appears to Sarah's maidservant Hagar (Genesis 16:7-14), and also prevents Abraham from sacrificing his son Isaac (Genesis 22:11-18). He appears to Moses in the burning bush (Exodus 3:2-6), and speaks clearly to the Israelites as God (Judges 2:1-4). There are other places where the angel appears, but does not speak as God. It is probable too that he is the 'angel of God's presence' who saved the people in the wilderness (Isaiah 63:9).

It would seem that this 'god-angel' is identified with Christ in Malachi 3:1. 'I will send my messenger, who will prepare the way before me. Then suddenly the Lord you are seeking will come to his temple; the messenger of the covenant, whom you desire, will come' (NIV).

Because both Hebrew and the Greek use the same word for *messenger* and *angel*, and we have to decide from the context which is the better translation in any particular instance. So while the former here is the human messenger – John the Baptist – the second is undoubtedly *the* angel of the covenant – here Jesus Christ.

In speaking of the Trinity we have to remember that while all Three are involved in the actions of any One, each Person tends to fulfil a particular function: the Father remains the Centre in heaven; the Son has the propensity to become Man on earth; the Spirit to become the unseen Executor in the church and in the Christian.

So it makes sense to see any pre-Christian appearance of God as that of Christ. But no such *appearance* could redeem mankind. For redemption, the Son must be born into the human race and become one with us.[*]

---

[*] The Virgin Birth and other teachings that are basic to the Christian faith are looked at in *The Simplicity of the Incarnation*, a previously unpublished book by J Stafford Wright, ISBN 9-780-9525-9564-9, also from White Tree Publishing 2011. See front of this book for details.

14: Miracles

Some events in the Bible seem unusual to us simply because they belong to a different time and different way of life. We may need help to understand them, help such as is available in books telling us about life in Bible times.

The mysteries discussed now may seem to be unlikely, and some people may even regard them as impossible. It is worth remembering that these phenomena all appear in life outside the Bible, and our age has seen scepticism, credulity, and a willingness to examine strange happenings more closely.

Scepticism comes through drawing the boundaries of knowledge too tightly, so that we automatically reject certain happenings as impossible. Credulity comes when we are anxious to swallow anything exciting. Contemporary willingness to examine the mysterious is easily seen in the huge number of books, articles and broadcasts which discuss strange phenomena of the past and present.

Many people – both Christian and non-Christian – are today uneasy about accepting some of the unusual events that both the Old and New Testaments record as if they really happened in history. The danger of an examination such as the one we are making in this book is that it gives the impression that the Bible is packed full of mysteries and unusual events, and that we are setting out to explain them without reference to God. But I believe more harm is done by living with a mind which simply sweeps all these mysterious events under the carpet.

We cannot *prove* that the events examined actually happened. The best we can hope to do is to show that modern experience and thought can make the event appear reasonable and not incredible. Granted that God can work in ways that we cannot understand, yet as we have seen earlier, there are also times when he draws out faculties which he has implanted in human beings, and thus enables them to bring about supernormal results for his purposes.

If we can find men and women doing similar supernormal things for their own purposes, we can reasonably see that God can use the same channels in Christians.

Miracles are the most obvious examples of Bible mysteries. God is no mere conjuror who does such brilliant tricks that no one can guess how he does them. That is why it is not enough to define a miracle simply as an unusual event which cannot be accounted for by natural laws alone. We need to include the word 'significant' somewhere in the definition. Of the two Greek words for *miracle* in the New Testament, the more common one means simply *sign*; the other means *power* or *work of power*.

Biblical miracles are never haphazard. They are always significant and meaningful. The majority are works of power from God, but occasionally they originate from other spiritual beings who intend to produce happenings which are significantly against God.

Jesus Christ told us not to be deceived by the claims of false Messiahs and false prophets, even if they were supported by signs and wonders (Matthew 24:24; Mark 13:22). Similarly, in the book of Revelation one of the symbolic beasts deceives mankind by his miracles (Revelation 13:13), as do certain demonic spirits. The apostle Paul also speaks of the 'counterfeit miracles, signs and wonders' of the 'lawless one' (2 Thessalonians 2:9 NIV). The significance of these miracles lies in their purpose of inspiring devotion to the deceptive spiritual leaders.

We have to realise that miraculous happenings are not of themselves proof of God's approval of some person or movement. At the same time we cannot automatically assume that a miracle associated with a movement, of which we do not ourselves approve, is a work of the Devil. Even if it is not of God, it might still be due to some psychic power.

Our understanding of miracles must include miracles of synchronisation. An event may have an explanation which is fully consistent with the observed sequence of cause and effect, yet it may still be classed as a miracle. For example, the crossing of the Red Sea by the Israelites at the exodus from Egypt was made possible, as the Bible says, by a strong east wind, which perhaps combined with the tides to expose a causeway, with water on each side acting as a wall to stop the people being out-flanked.

It is not necessary to interpret the poetry of the biblical account to mean there were high walls of water on either side (Exodus 14:21-22; 15:8). In the same way, 'a wind from the Lord' brought quails to the camp of the Israelites during their wilderness wanderings, just when they were desperate for food (Numbers 11:31).

If these incidents are explained as natural phenomena, the miracle lies in the fact that they occurred at the very moment when God's people needed it.

But does the Bible justify our attempting to make a special category labelled 'miracles', and then trying to find some satisfactory definition for the term we have used? Are we trying to draw too tight a boundary between Nature and Supernature? The Bible is a record of the mighty acts of God, and these acts appear in the realm of both the natural and the supernatural. Are we called to distinguish between them?

A clear example is found in the healings recorded in the Bible, and particularly the healings attributed to Jesus. These healings demonstrated that he was the promised Messiah, but the records of the healings do not justify us holding that they were *all* performed by virtue of his divine nature. Some *could* have been brought about through suggestion, others through his use of latent powers which everyone possesses in rudimentary form, and would certainly be possessed by one who was perfect man. It may then be useless to try to fix boundaries which God has not encouraged us to fix.

Yet even if we do not attempt to define miracles, we must face the alleged fact that events have happened which come into head-on collision with the probabilities which science treats as virtual certainties. When such events occur, those who experience them usually refer to them as miracles. It then becomes a matter for intelligent investigation whether the event is the work of some unseen spiritual being, and if so whether this being is God, angel, or devil. Alternatively, the event may be wholly the result of human action, where the doer makes use consciously or unconsciously of psychic powers which are inherent in him or her.

If these powers operate through non-physical channels, they are not altogether open to investigation by the physical scientists. There is another possibility: that the miraculous event is a blend of spiritual and human activity. God, or some spiritual entity, temporarily possesses a person in such a way as to direct his latent psychic powers into psychic activity which appears as a miracle.

Four events can be ascribed to the direct action of God alone. These are: the original creation of the universe; the incarnation of Jesus Christ; the resurrection of Jesus Christ; and the final acts of God at the time of the end. We do not, of course, mean that other events may not be due to God's direct action.

When it comes to accepting the stories of miracles, even those who believe that 'something happened', may claim that the event is misinterpreted as a work of God. We have earlier referred to the Gospel records that Jesus allowed a host of demons to leave a man they possessed, and ordered them to enter a herd of swine which immediately rushed down the hillside into the lake (Matthew 8:28-32; Mark 5:1-13; Luke 8:26-33).

Jesus understood the ways of evil spirits when suddenly cast out, and he must have had a good reason for sending them into the swine. Possibly there was the risk that they would enter into members of the excited crowd of bystanders; but whatever the reason, we need not adopt the re-writing of the story suggested by those who do not believe in the existence of spirits – namely that the ravings of the madman frightened the pigs.

Similarly, the miracle of the loaves and fishes has been

watered down by some scholars. It has been suggested that the act of the boy who produced his loaves and fishes led the crowd as a whole to produce the food which each had kept to himself until that point (John 6:1-14).

These are re-writings of the original stories to meet objections by the modern reader. Others dismiss Bible mysteries on the ground that they are mere folklore. Commentators are too ready to write off as folk tales such incidents as the floating axe-head (2 Kings 6:4-7), Balaam's ass (Numbers 22:28-30), and the three men preserved in the fiery furnace (Daniel 3). Anyone aware of psychic physical phenomena will at least consider these events as possible, as we shall see later.

A seer such as Balaam evidently possessed the gifts of clairvoyance and clairaudience, by which psychic perceptions impinge on the consciousness in the form of visions or voices. When his donkey brayed indignantly, God conveyed its meaning to Balaam in the form of a human voice. There are other similar happenings in the Bible.

On one occasion the voice of God was heard from heaven when Jesus was praying.

'Now my soul is troubled, and what shall I say? "Father, save me from this hour"? No, it was for this very reason I came to this hour. Father, glorify your name!' Then a voice came from heaven, 'I have glorified it, and will glorify it again.' The crowd that was there and heard it said it had thundered; others said an angel had spoken to him. Jesus said, 'This voice was for your benefit, not mine' (John 12:27-30 NIV).

When Jesus spoke to Saul on the road to Damascus it is clear that those with him heard simply a sound from heaven; only Paul heard this sound as words (Acts 9:3-9; 22:6-9).

We may conclude that we are not justified in making the distinction that some do, between so-called 'nature-miracles' of the Bible, and the more personal miracles such as healings which are easier to believe in the light of modern psychology and experiences of healing.

Ultimately, the reason for attempting to show the credibility of Bible miracles is that they are largely bound up with the supreme revelation of God in Christ. The miracles of the Old Testament are part of the preparation for his coming, and from part of the Book which he clearly accepted as the inspired and true Word of God. They are not scattered haphazard through the pages of the Bible, as we might expect if they were merely fictitious. They occur chiefly in three periods.

The first period was when God was bringing his people out of Egypt and wished to impress upon them his power and his ability to save. In the light of the constant pull of more attractive and easy-going heathen deities, God made his presence and power felt in a way which could not be denied.

The second period was when God began to speak through his prophets. For example, when there was a deliberate attempt to introduce a strong rival deity, Baal-Melkart, God gave power to Elijah and Elisha to authenticate their words by miracles.

After this there were few miracles, until the coming of Jesus the Messiah, and the launching of the church on its world-wide mission.

15: Body Mysteries

Undoubtedly, under special conditions, the human body can have its powers amazingly extended. The biblical hero Samson is shown in such a light in the book of Judges, chapters 13 to 16. It is assumed that he was a man of normal strength and health. Yet on almost every occasion where he is recorded as carrying out some supernormal act of strength, the Bible states, 'The Spirit of the LORD came powerfully upon him.' For instance, Judges 14:19 reads, 'Then the Spirit of the LORD came powerfully upon him. He went down to Ashkelon, struck down thirty of their men, stripped them of their belongings and gave their clothes to those who had explained the riddle' (NIV). This is yet another example of how the Lord works through extended human capacities.

The account of Samson in the Bible names so many actual places that there is every reason to regard him as a historical figure rather than a legendary hero. Certainly his flawed personality does not suggest his being the fabrication of some pious theological writer. He was a man used by God to stem the Philistine encroachments into the territory of the Tribe of Dan; his power and effectiveness depending directly upon his continuing witness to God. He was a lifelong adherent to the Nazarite religious vow, symbolised by uncut hair and teetotalism.

Yet there is no need for us to exaggerate Samson's strength. The Bible records his killing one thousand men in a single raid, 'The Spirit of the LORD came powerfully upon him. The ropes on his arms became like charred flax, and the bindings dropped from his hands. Finding a fresh jawbone of a donkey, he grabbed it and struck down a thousand men' (Judges 15:14-15 NIV). However, recent studies have shown that in some instances noughts have been added to numbers to make some of the unusually large figures recorded in the Old Testament[*]. So it could well be that an over-enthusiastic copyist added at least one extra nought to the number of men Samson is recorded as having massacred.

In other instances where very large numbers are found in the Old Testament, scholars have pointed out that the Hebrew word translated *thousand* may be translated as

---

[*] "There is evidence that the Old Testament text is on the whole marvellously well preserved. There is also evidence from the parallel passages in Samuel, Kings and Chronicles and (especially) in Ezra 2 and Nehemiah 7 that numbers were peculiarly difficult to transmit accurately. We have instances of extra noughts being added to a number: 2 Samuel 10:18 reads '700 chariots', 1 Chronicles 19:18 reads '7,000'. A digit can drop out: 2 Kings 24:8 gives the age of Jehoiachin on accession as 18, whereas 2 Chronicles 36:9 gives it as 8. An entire numeral can drop out ... And there are other errors of copying, many of which are easily explained" (John Wenham). (Alexander and Alexander, *Eerdmans' Handbook to the Bible,* 1973, page 191.)

chief, military group, family or *clan**.

Another account of Samson's exploits as a strong man almost certainly needs similar modification. In this instance Samson was trapped in the city of Gaza, but escaped by night by taking down the city gates. We are told, 'He lifted them to his shoulders and carried them to the top of the hill that faces Hebron' (Judges 16:3 NIV). It has been assumed that he carried them under cover of night the entire 38 miles [61 km] from Gaza to Hebron – a long enough distance *without* the burden of a pair of city gates. However, the Hebrew can mean 'the hill that looks across to Hebron'.

I wrote to the Mayor of Gaza to ask whether such a hill exists. He replied, 'I am glad to inform you that it is possible to see the Hebron mountains from the hills close to Gaza, especially from Munter Hill [Ali el-Muntar].' From this information I assume it was up this hill that Samson carried the gates. There is no merit in adopting a difficult interpretation of the Bible when without twisting the text a simpler one is available.

Samson's pulling down of the pillars which supported the temple of Dagon in Gaza (Judges 16:23-30) is scarcely comprehensible if we regard them as pillars similar to

---

* "In the modern Hebrew Bible all numbers are written out in full, but for a long time the text was written without vowels. The absence of vowels made it possible to confuse two words which are crucial to this problem: *'eleph* and *'alluph*. Without vowel points these words look identical: *'lp. 'eleph* is the ordinary word for 'thousand', but it can also be used in a variety of other senses: e.g. 'family' (Judges 6:15, Revised Version) or 'clan' (Zechariah 9:7; 12:5-6, Revised Standard Version) or perhaps a military unit. *'alluph* is used for the 'chieftains' of Edom (Genesis 36:15–43); probably for a commander of a military 'thousand'; and almost certainly for the professional, fully-armed soldier" (John Wenham). (Alexander and Alexander, *Eerdmans' Handbook to the Bible,* 1973, page 191.)

those of a medieval cathedral. But the pillars in question were almost certainly made of wood, resting on stone bases. The Bible describes the scene of destruction as an open court surrounded by broad balconies on which people crowded to watch Samson the Israelite captive being humiliated below.

These balconies presumably had pillars to support them, but there were also two main pillars. When Samson pushed these main pillars off their bases a domino effect seems to have brought all the balconies crashing into the courtyard below, causing terrible carnage.

There are other strange extensions of the body's properties mentioned in the Bible, in addition to purely physical strength. There is for example our Lord's forty-day fast in the wilderness, recorded in Matthew 4:1-11. Some people might claim that he was able to fast for such a long period because he was divine, but in fact it was because Jesus had a human body which needed food that the fast was a true one. He refused to turn stones into bread for himself, though later in his ministry he multiplied loaves and fishes to feed a hungry crowd.

Many people have engaged in prolonged fasts, but rarely under such conditions. An attempt to follow Christ's example was made by the Indian Christian Sadhu Sundar Singh in 1912. Nobody, not even the Sadhu himself, knows how long his fast had lasted when he was discovered in a state of collapse, unrecognizable even to his friends, but on a great spiritual 'high'.

The Bible also records mysterious physical escapes from certain death. There is the story of Daniel in the lions' den – or more precisely, the lion pit, recorded in Daniel 6. King Darius the Mede was persuaded by Daniel's rivals to throw him into a lion pit whose bottom entrance was sealed with the royal seal so that nobody could release him. It was improbable that the hungry lions would spare him, but in the morning Daniel told Darius, 'My God sent his angel and he shut the mouths of the lions. They have not hurt me, because I was found innocent in his sight.'

There is no need to conjure up the picture of an angel running round muzzling the lions. The angel was able to use the dominion over living creatures which God has given to man; as Psalm 8 says, 'You made him ruler over the works of your hands ... all the beasts of the field.' This is a potential which we see actualised in certain people who seem to have a natural affinity and understanding with members of the animal kingdom – even, as TV has shown, lions and tigers. Under the influence of the angel, Daniel and the lions were drawn together in harmony.

The other great mystery in the book of Daniel is the survival of Shadrach, Meshach and Abednego in the burning fiery furnace, recorded in chapter 3. This story is frequently written off as a propaganda fable, allegedly written [four hundred years later, in the 2nd century BC] to inspire the Jews to resist the demands of their brutal persecutor, Antiochus Epiphanes. This is an easy assumption to make, unless carefully considered.

The three men who resisted Nebuchadnezzar's demands were miraculously delivered, whereas the Jews who resisted Antiochus were put to death. If I had been inventing the story I should have made the three die in the fire, but be caught up immediately to be with God. Otherwise it would be rather like telling the hopeful story of Cinderella to a poor girl who had just been jilted by a rich lover. The biblical story of the three survivors would only intensify the complaint, 'Why does it happen to them, and not me?'

I have a photograph of a Calcutta fakir named Jatoo Bhai dancing barefoot in a blazing fire. I have another photograph taken immediately afterwards, showing that neither the soles of his feet nor even his long yellow pantaloons were scorched.

Accounts of firewalking by reputable observers come from many parts of the world. When a New Zealand magistrate and doctor hung a thermometer six feet above a firewalkers' trench, the solder melted. In 1921 in Madras, a demonstration was given in front of the Roman Catholic bishop of Mysore and the local Maharajah. A Muslim fakir organised the event and claimed he was drawing all the pain into his own body. After several volunteers had walked unscathed through the burning embers, members of a Christian brass band marched through unharmed, playing their musical instruments.

Because such events are so extraordinary we like more instances of them. A member of staff from the British Museum, a Dr WT Brigham, agreed to walk with three local magicians across glowing lava on the South Sea island of South Kona. They walked barefoot, but Dr Brigham refused to go across without his boots on, although the magicians warned him the boots would not be protected. In the event, he had only covered a few steps when his socks and boots were left in charred ruins on the lava, although his feet and remaining clothes were completely unmarked.

If all this seems rather far away, the [Scottish] medium DD Home [1833-1886], who was never detected in fraud, used to take burning embers from the fire and blow them still hotter in his cupped hands. He even put a burning coal on another person's head with no harmful result. Sir William Crookes and Lord Adare who observed Home regularly in broad daylight, also saw him hold coals in a handkerchief which was completely unsinged. On one occasion Home even placed his head in an open fire.

In 1793, during the Jansenist religious disturbances in Paris, a girl used to lie in a rigid trance over a blazing fire; neither she nor the sheet covering her were burnt. She was observed by representatives of the church and by free-thinkers, both wishing to discredit this and other Jansenist wonders.

It is important to emphasize that no treatment is given to the feet beforehand, and that the subject's clothes are not burnt. [There also that there reliable reports of severe injuries and even death.] Generally there is some form of preliminary ceremony, and sometimes there is a director who claims to draw any effects of the fire into himself. But if the participants are in a hypnotic trance, who hypnotizes their clothes?

Let us return now to Nebuchadnezzar's burning fiery furnace. The three men clearly experienced something far beyond anything we have mentioned; but we might expect God to go beyond, though not producing an effect with no parallels.

The Bible records that the three men were joined in the fire by one 'like a son of the gods'. Could this be the equivalent of the 'director' who draws the pain into himself? The book of Daniel also says that though the ropes that bound the men were burnt, their clothes were unsinged. It all fits.

16: Prediction

Outside the Bible there are two sets of celebrated long-term predictions. One consists of a series of descriptions of successive popes, supposedly written by Malachy a twelfth-century archbishop of Armagh. Some of these epigrams clearly fit particular popes; the 'shepherd and navigator' could refer to Pope John XXIII's links with maritime Venice, and 'Flower of Flowers' could point to Pope Paul VI's coat-of-arms, three fleurs-de-lis. Other epigrams are less easily interpreted.

The other famous set of predictions is that by Nostradamus. Michel de Nostradame was a French Hebrew-Christian born in 1503. He was trained as a doctor and appears to have been a competent medical practitioner. His fame, however, rests on his book known as *Centuries,* which was published in a number of editions from 1555 till his death in 1566.

Nostradamus' book consists of sets of four-line verses written in French and Latin doggerel, in which he aimed to foretell the future up to the year 2000[*]. Some of the predictions are so startling that the casual reader might

---

[*] With 'a great king of terror' coming from the sky in July 1999, which clearly didn't happen, although it sent some interpreters of Nostradamus into a frenzy as that date approached.

wonder whether they were embellished after the event.

This was my suspicion, so I spent an afternoon in the British Museum consulting an edition of *Centuries* dated 1605. I found that the verses really do stand there as they are normally quoted[*].

The quatrains of Nostradamus usually appear obscure and nonsensical. He claimed that he deliberately made them opaque, since otherwise the civil and church leaders of his day would have condemned his predictions. Nostradamus undoubtedly foresaw the French Revolution of 1789. Take the striking example of quatrain IX 34:

Le part solus mary sera mitré:
Retour: Conflict passera sur le thuille
Par cinq cens: un trahyr sera titré
Narbon: et Saulce par coutaux avons d'huille.

Nostradamus writer, James Laver, translates this:

The husband alone will be mitred.
Return. A conflict will pass over the tiles by five hundred: a traitor will be titled Narbonne: and from Saulce we have oil in quarts.

We may quarrel with details of this translation, and the 1605 edition has slight differences of punctuation. But the main words are not disputed. The first two lines could refer to the mob that invaded the Tuileries and made Louis XVI wear the red cap of liberty, which is not unlike a mitre. This

---

[*] Quoted in reliable publications, not in sensational publications from Victorian times onwards, nor nowadays on the internet, where verses *have* been misquoted and even fabricated.

may not sound too convincing, but when we arrive at the two proper names we have to take notice.

The Comte de Narbonne was Louis XVI's War Minister, who was intriguing with the revolutionaries, and so a 'traitor'. The other man was actually called Sauce. He was the Procureur of Varennes, and he arrested Louis XVI during his attempted flight. Sauce was by trade a grocer and chandler. Naturally the more obscure parts of Nostradamus' predictions have been a happy hunting-ground for generations of searchers, but it seems he foresaw aerial warfare:

> *Sera laisse feu vif, mort caché,*
> *Dedans les globes horrible espouvantable.*
> *De nuict a classe cite en poudre lasché*
> *La cite a feu, l'ennemy favorable.*

Laver translates:

> *There will be loosed living fire and death hidden*
> *in globes, horrible! frightful!*
> *By night hostile forces will reduce the city*
> *to powder,*
> *The fact that it is already on fire being favourable*
> *to the enemy.*

Commentators on the *Centuries* of Nostradamus have traced likely predictions about the history of France, and Hitler discovered himself there under the name of Hister[*].

---

[*] Hister was a name for the lower Danube area at the time of Nostradamus, and the majority of commentators today take this as being the intended meaning. Others point out that this was the area where Hitler was born.

Predictions of a similar kind occur in the Bible. For example, the exile and return of Israel are foretold in Leviticus 26. It is significant that the exile is spoken of as dependent upon the future behaviour of the nation.

The future is foretold in the book of Daniel which describes the persecution of Israel and the desecration of the temple under Antiochus Epiphanes some 400 years later (Daniel 11). Why should this have been foretold so long beforehand? For the sufferers involved it was an encouragement to know that all had been foreseen by God, and that deliverance would come. It was in fact the last great time of testing before the coming of the Messiah.

Nostradamus names historical figures before their time. Similarly, a biblical prophet said that Josiah would be the name of the king who would put down idolatry, three centuries before Josiah lived (1 Kings 13:2).

Precognition may help shed light on the problem of the authorship of the second half of the book of Isaiah. Very few scholars today believe that Isaiah himself wrote chapters 40 to 66. But the first and second halves of the book are linked by the prediction, in chapter 39:6, that there would be an exile in Babylon. The remaining chapters consist of words of comfort for the people when they found themselves in Babylon.

A feature of Isaiah 40 to 66 is the continued assertion by God that he can predict the future. For example he challenged the pagan idols to predict what the future held (41:21-24); he declares 'new things ... before they spring into being' (42:9). But where is the proof of his claims? Here if anywhere we should expect to find a really startling prediction. We have it, in the naming of Cyrus as the man who would set the people free (Isaiah 44:28; 45:1)![*]

I believe Isaiah wrote these final chapters under God's inspiration to encourage the captives when they found that God had foreseen their plight years before, and had prepared a deliverer for them. *Anyone* could have made a guess about Cyrus as deliverer – once he was coming into prominence as conqueror!

Sometime early in the twentieth century somebody coined the clever-sounding epigram: 'The prophets were forthtellers, not foretellers.' In fact this is a stupid half-truth. Biblical prophets were both forthtellers *and* foretellers, giving both short term and long-term predictions. We have already noted examples.

The prophet Micaiah predicted that the expedition to retake Ramoth-gilead would be disastrous (1 Kings 22), and Jeremiah predicted that the false prophet Hananiah would die within a year (Jeremiah 28:16-17). Both of these short-term prophecies came true. Long-term predictions appear more difficult, but they *are* found in the Bible. Jeremiah foretold in 605 BC that the Babylonian rule over Palestine would last seventy years, which was in round figures correct.

There also occur long-term predictions of the Messiah, of which we are reminded in Handel's oratorio. Jesus himself explained to his disciples how all the Scriptures

---

[*] In *What Is Man* (Paternoster Press, 1955), the author explores this controversy on Isaiah's prophecy in greater detail, and ends with the following wording: '*Isaiah 40 to 55 contains such remarkable descriptions of the Lord Jesus Christ, that to be consistent, one should date these chapters AD rather than BC! This digression is not intended as an attack on all modern theologians. Some of them are already realizing that the findings of psychical research have a significance for biblical study, but they have not yet seen clearly the significance of the fact of detailed precognition.*'

contained references to himself (Luke 24:27,44-47). The apostle Peter also points out that the prophets were led to say things which they could not understand in their contemporary situation, 'trying to find out the time and circumstances to which the Spirit of Christ in them was pointing when he predicted the sufferings of the Messiah' (1 Peter 1:10-12).

It is often difficult to prove that an alleged prediction was actually made beforehand and not written up afterwards. This is particularly so with short-term predictions. Of course, anyone can claim that Jeremiah's prediction of Hananiah's death within a year was subsequently written in by Baruch the scribe who probably collected and recorded Jeremiah's words. The long-term predictions of the Messiah are different, since we possess the prophecies that we know were written down centuries earlier.

17: Dreams

When we have records of unusual happenings in the past, we can try to assess their probability by comparing similar events today. We can also compare them with other well-established historical happenings. Thus, however difficult it is to suggest a model of the future that can be perceived in the present, there are enough examples to show there are people who have seen, and do see, future events.

An often-quoted modern example concerns the Aberfan disaster of 1966, when a Welsh school was swallowed up with great loss of life by a slide of coal waste from the mountain above. Afterwards psychiatrist and researcher Dr John Baker advertised in the press for anyone who appeared to have received a premonition of the disaster. In reply he received seventy-six letters, of which three were completely definite and could be authenticated, since the premonitions had been recounted to another person beforehand.

Most of these premonitions of Aberfan came in dreams. Similarly, one source of the prophets' inspiration in the Bible was the dream, as we have seen. 'When a prophet of the LORD is among you, I reveal myself to him in visions, I speak to him in dreams.' (Numbers 12:6 NIV). 'Let the prophet who has a dream tell his dream' (Jeremiah 23:28 NIV).

In the Bible, precognitive dreams are full of symbols, and need to be interpreted. Joseph dreamed about his family under the form of the sun, moon and stars bowing down before him (Genesis 37:5-11). In prison he interpreted the butler's dream of a vine with three branches: the butler would be restored from prison in three days. The baker's dream of birds eating the cakes from three baskets meant death for him in three days (Genesis 46). Pharaoh's dream of seven thin cows eating up seven fat ones meant seven years of famine following seven years of plenty (Genesis 41).

The Israelite Gideon heard a Midianite enemy telling his dream of a barley-loaf falling on a Midianite tent and overturning it. His friend rightly interpreted the dream as referring to Gideon's coming destructive attack on the Midianites (Judges 7:13-14).

Nowadays it is the psychiatrist who interprets the symbolism of his patient's dreams – and these dreams often seem to disclose present inner needs. It is likely that many of us who are not psychic have precognitive dreams, although the dream fades so rapidly on waking that we do not normally remember it.

One night I dreamt of a child playing with a yo-yo. The yo-yo craze was long-since dead, and I had not seen one in years. The next day in another part of my home town I saw a little child playing with a yo-yo. After that, I didn't see another for months.

Someone I know well has occasional precognitive dreams. She is the wife of a clergyman, and when her husband was considering a new job she dreamt of a large white building with pillars at the doorway and a passage basement below, with a pile of planks, barrels and other rubbish lying outside the front door. She was welcomed in her dream by a Mrs E, whom she knew slightly.

As her husband was considering a teaching post at a college, which she had never seen, he asked her to describe the dream-building before she went to see the college concerned. The description tallied with the college, except for the planks and rubbish. Moreover her first impression on meeting the principal's wife was, 'She reminds me of Mrs E.'

After they had been at the college for some months she came up the drive one day to find that the contents of the basement were being cleared out, and planks, barrels and rubbish were lying beside the doorway awaiting clearance.

It is rare that a dream of the future is as clear as this. What seems likely is that future elements go to form the ideas of a dream just as elements of the past. For example, if I had a dream of the yo-yo on the night *after* I had seen the child playing with it, no one would have doubted that the actual (past) event influenced my dream. But it may equally be that the actual (future) event influenced my dream[*].

Dreams have been studied scientifically, especially in the dream laboratory at the Maimonides Medical Center in

---

[*] Some Christians form the habit of praying for people they dream about, before the dream fades, whether or not the dream appears to have precognitive qualities. For this reason alone, it is worth recalling our dreams on waking.

Brooklyn New York. Tests have revealed ESP in dreams, including precognition.

We were led to look at precognitive dreams by the Bible accounts, but in considering precognition there is no need to restrict ourselves to dreams. In Britain, the Scots, Welsh and Irish commonly accept they have the gift of second sight, as do gypsies and others. In modern America, Jeane Dixon [1904-1997], a devout Roman Catholic, has made some striking predictions, both of national events, such as the assassination of President Kennedy, and also individual warnings, such as the crash of a friend's plane. However, she has also had some obvious failures in prediction.

Certainly some people have a fairly clear foreknowledge of events, though this does not necessarily commit us to a belief in inevitable fate. The Frenchman, Eugene Osty [1874-1938], was in constant touch with mediums and others to see how far they could predict his future. He found they made accurate forecasts about short-term happenings, but a mixture of right and wrong about more distant events. He concluded that the distance allowed for alternative decisions that he might take. Precognition can act as a warning, so that somebody can intervene and stop the event from taking place as it occurred in, say, a dream.

Although such short-term predictions rarely occur in the Bible, these examples show that prediction is possible. Long-term predictions however do occur in the Bible. King Nebuchadnezzar's dream of a great image, symbolising the three empires that would follow Babylon, occurs in the book of Daniel chapter 2.

Daniel, who interpreted the king's dream himself, had more detailed visions concerning these empires in chapters 7 to 12. He lived in the sixth century BC under the Babylonian Empire and the early Persian Empire. He told Nebuchadnezzar that there would be three empires after him, namely [what we now call] the Medo-Persian, the Greek and the Roman.

Daniel's own visions, as we have seen, dwelt upon the desecration of the temple in 168 BC by the Greek Antiochus Epiphanes, but his visions also led up to the Messiah who would arise during the Roman rule. There are some uncertainties over the exact translation of 9:25-27, but it is possible to see a dating to the coming of 'the Anointed One, the ruler' who 'will be cut off' and 'put an end to sacrifice and offering', a perfect picture of Jesus Christ. The picture is interwoven with another destroyer, Nero.

One of the problems about prediction is interpretation, especially when history repeats itself. At various periods of history, such as during World War II, some Christians discovered contemporary figures such as Hitler and Mussolini in Daniel's visions. Jesus himself, in speaking of the coming destruction of Jerusalem, said, 'When you see standing in the holy place "the abomination that causes desolation", spoken of through the prophet Daniel ...' (Matthew 24:15 NIV). Many people think there will be a further fulfilment in the Antichrist, the temple being now the Christian church.

The other difficulty about Daniel's prophecies concerns the detailed description, not only of the empires, but of the actual movements of Antiochus in Daniel 11. Could such events really be foretold four hundred years beforehand? Are such predictions so impossible that we must assume they were written by some person other than Daniel, after they had occurred? As we have seen, such long-term predictions occur outside the Bible too, in Nostradamus and Malachy.

There is one date in Daniel which is either an incredible coincidence, or a true prediction from God. It is a figure which is given, bearing no relation to surrounding numbers: 'Blessed is the one who waits for and reaches the end of the 1,335 days' (Daniel 12:12).

In 1917 the British General Allenby captured Jerusalem, and ended the Turkish rule, thus beginning the cycle of events that led to the return of the Jews and the setting up of the State of Israel. In the Muslim calendar (the Turks were Muslims) the year was 1335, the year given by Daniel.

And that is not all. The Arabs pronounced Allenby's name as Al Nebi, which is the Arabic for The Prophet. In addition, there was an old Arabic prophecy 'when the Nile flows into Palestine, then shall the prophet (Al Nebi) from the west drive the Turk from Jerusalem.' The troops laid a pipeline from Egypt to a point north of Gaza and pumped Nile water into Palestine. Here is the coming together of remarkable biblical and secular predictions.

For reference:
James Laver: *Nostradamus,* Penguin, 1952
J. W. Dunne, *An Experiment with Time,* 1927
Osty: *Supernatural Faculties in Man,* 1923
Vivian Gilbert: *The Romance of the Last Crusade,* Appleton, 1926

18: Prophets

What is so unusual about prophets? Aren't there prophets for the modern age – men who speak out boldly against current evils, or who lead campaigns for a good cause? Aren't their words 'prophetic'? Certainly they speak out about issues similar to those which concerned the prophets of the Bible. But such people are not prophets in the biblical sense. The Bible puts prophets into a different category from teachers and preachers, however outspoken these may be.

Ezra and Nehemiah both campaigned against wrong, and championed what was right; but they are never called prophets. On the other hand, relatively quiet characters such as Abraham, Isaac and Jacob are described by God as prophets, when he tells their enemies, 'Do not touch my anointed ones; do my prophets no harm' (Psalm 105:15).

What is the difference? A prophet is one to whom God speaks directly. Again and again the prophets introduce their pronouncements with words like, 'The word of the Lord came to me', 'The Lord said to me', and consequently 'Thus says the Lord'.

There is an exact illustration of the status of a prophet in Exodus 7:1-2. Moses tells God that he is a poor speaker, so God replies that Moses shall be in the position of God, and Aaron shall be in the position of Moses' prophet. Moses will tell Aaron the words of God, and Aaron will transmit them to Pharaoh. Thus, a prophet is one who hears and then transmits what he hears.

Most of us have been familiar since childhood with the story of Samuel who as a young man helped in the temple. One night he heard a voice calling him by name, and thought he was being called by Eli the High Priest. This happened three times and each time he found he was mistaken. The third time Eli guessed that the voice was that of the Lord. Next time, Samuel responded to the voice: 'Speak, for your servant is listening,' and he received his first message as a prophet (1 Samuel 3).

Sometimes a vision accompanied the voice. If as seems likely, Isaiah 6 describes the call of the prophet, he saw the Lord exalted on a throne high up in the temple and heard the voice of the Lord commissioning him. Jeremiah at his commissioning had a vision of the Lord touching his mouth. Ezekiel had a vision of God in his glory and was shown a scroll of prophetic messages which he was to eat.

A sceptic may object that hearing voices is a symptom of schizophrenia. But to say that the good sense of the prophetic messages emanated from schizophrenics makes no sense at all.

Spiritualists claim that they too hear supernatural voices and see visions of the departed. But spiritualists do not believe that their communications are the voice of God, whereas the prophets did not believe that their communications were from anyone else *but* God.

Yet in both instances we are dealing with the mysterious realm of the unconscious, which includes clairvoyance and clairaudience. God does not speak to the prophets in words that other people can hear, or show visions that other people can see. The visions do not emanate from the conscious mind or from sense perception, although the conscious mind interprets them. The prophet tells what he has heard or seen; the spiritualist medium does the same.

The Bible itself makes a connection when it notes that a prophet might be called a seer (1 Samuel 9:9). A seer is simply 'one who sees' [a see-er], but the suggestion is that his vision is inward, as when Balaam says of himself that he speaks 'the oracle of one whose eyes see clearly ... and whose eyes are opened' (Numbers 24:15-16 NIV).

The word *seer* is used a number of times in the Bible, but generally in the sense of an inspired adviser. Thus in 1 Samuel 9, Saul and his servant go to consult a seer about their lost asses. David was advised by court seers such as Gad (2 Samuel 24:11). Gad and Iddo under Solomon kept court records (1 Chronicles 29:29; 2 Chronicles 9:29).

We know very little about the mechanism behind such phenomena as clairvoyance and clairaudience. An imbalance of the mind may open up the unconscious to voices and visions, as with schizophrenia. The medium, often in trance or semi-trance, passes beyond normal consciousness into a new awareness. Neither becomes a prophet in the biblical sense. But can we not say that God, who created and understands the beyond-consciousness, can use it as a vehicle for his communication with certain chosen people – his prophets?

We can see from the records of prophecy in the Old Testament that God communicated messages of rebuke, encouragement, diagnosis and prediction; but at the heart of his messages was a call to loyalty to himself and faith in himself.

There is a striking example of clairvoyance and clair-audience in 2 Kings 6:8-12. Elisha is able to tell the King of Israel the decisions that the King of Syria made in conference with his officers. God stimulated and directed the faculties of inner vision that were latent in Elisha, with the result that he made no mistake. Human faculties of this sort are not always accurate and cannot be turned on at will. It is rumoured that the USSR has been attempting [in 1984] to mobilise clairvoyance and clairaudience against the West, in the same way as Elisha against Syria[*].

It is helpful at this stage to look at Jeremiah's diagnosis of true and false prophecy in Jeremiah 23. God says, 'I did not speak to these prophets, yet they prophesied' (verse 21). "I have heard what the prophets say who prophesy lies in my name. They say, 'I had a dream! I had a dream!'" (verse 25 NIV). It is clear that Jeremiah recognises that an apparently prophetic message may come by a dream, or it may come from the heart (here, the subconscious). It may be falsely assumed to be from God, although God may speak through a dream which conveys the true word of God (verse 28). Jeremiah himself dreamed a prophecy of the future blessing of his people, after which he says, 'There-upon I awoke, and looked around, and my sleep had been pleasant to me' (Jeremiah 31:26).

The message of God comes from a deep level, beyond the purely conscious mind. But from this deep level may come messages which are not from God at all. In Jeremiah 23, again God declares, 'Is not my word like fire, says the

---

[*] Similarly, the West against the USSR. America experimented officially with remote psychic viewing in their Stargate Project until the mid 1990s, and may still be doing it unofficially, along with other major world powers.

LORD, and like a hammer which breaks the rock in pieces?' (23:29). By contrast, the false prophets 'healed the wound of my people lightly, saying "Peace, peace," when there is no peace' (6:14 RSV).

Here they are associated with priests, and in Jeremiah 8:8-11 with the wise men, showing that prophets, true or false, were recognised as a separate class. They were seen to be speaking under some inner influence even though they could consciously record in writing, or dictate afterwards, what God had said to them or shown them. Although the false prophets seemed to be speaking under a similar inner inspiration, their words came from a source other than God.

God is the ultimate source of true prophetic inspiration, but this inspiration emerges through channels which he has placed in men and women. If God inspires a Handel to glorify his Messiah with an oratorio, he is using the same gift of music as is used by any composer. He does not create a new medium. If a Christian runs a marathon, he uses the same physical powers as are used by all the other runners. So when God inspires the prophets, he uses the non-conscious vehicle that often appears when the conscious mind is partly or wholly laid aside. A trance, with its accompanying effects, has similar features whether it is activated by the inner self, by some spirit being, or by God.

We do not know the depth of trance or ecstasy experienced by each prophet. However, it is certain that there was some mark which distinguished anyone who professed to be a prophet, from any ordinary speaker. But there was no way of telling from the manner of speech and behaviour whether a prophet was true or false, as the Old Testament records make quite clear.

19: True or False Prophets?

How do we distinguish a false prophet from a true one? Deuteronomy gives us two ways. In Deuteronomy 13:1-15 it is said that the false prophet may have the faculty of precognition, and may as a result foretell something which actually comes to pass. But if he claims his forecast as a sign that his hearers should turn from Jehovah to follow another god, he shows he is false. We are reminded of Christ's words that in the Christian era, 'false prophets will appear and perform great signs and wonders (Matthew 24:24). Wonders, miracles, including healings, do not authenticate a prophet.

The second test is diametrically opposite to the first. If any prophet speaking in the name of the Lord or of some other god gives a prediction that does not happen, he is not a true spokesman of the Lord (Deuteronomy 18:20-22). In this connection we may note that Jehovah's Witnesses have fixed wrong dates for the Millennial reign of Jesus Christ.

In the year 605 BC Jeremiah prophesied that Israel and Palestine would be under Babylonian domination for seventy years, after which the Jews who would be taken into exile would be allowed to return (Jeremiah 25:1-14; 29:10).

In fact, Cyrus of Persia conquered Babylon in 539, and the first return of the Jews was in 537 BC, which is near enough seventy years later.

There were several deportations of Jews to Babylon, the last being in 587 BC. Meanwhile, false prophets in Jerusalem and in Babylon said at first that the Babylonians would not invade at all (Jeremiah 14:13-16), and then foretold a speedy return from exile (Jeremiah 27:16-22; 29:1-28).

Jeremiah recounts an unpleasant encounter with a prophet named Hananiah, whom we mentioned earlier. Hananiah made a violent personal attack on Jeremiah (Jeremiah 28), and declared in the name of the Lord that the exile would be over within two years.

Jeremiah repeated what he had always foretold about a long exile, and in addition declared God's revelation that Hananiah would die before the year was out. The chapter ends, 'In that same year, in the seventh month, the prophet Hananiah died.' So we can see that Jeremiah demonstrated over both the long and the short term that he was a true prophet of the Lord.

In the Bible we occasionally encounter 'sons of the prophets'. This does not mean that the prophetic gift was necessarily inherited, although it may have been. The Hebrew terms *sons of* means *members of*. For instance, *sons of men* means *mankind*. References to sons of the prophets are generally to groups of prophets.

When Elijah was going on his final journey with Elisha they encountered 'the sons of the prophets' in Bethel and in Jericho (2 Kings 2 RSV; 'company of the prophets' NIV).

Later, Elisha had dealings with similar groups at Gilgal (2 Kings 4:38-44), and at an unnamed place where the prophets wanted to build an extension to their centre (2 Kings 6:1-7).

It is likely that groups of prophets lived and worshipped together. Saul, on his way home from being secretly anointed, met a group of prophets who were returning from worship. The Spirit of God came upon him and he joined them in prophesying. Saul had a similar experience later when he was pursuing David to kill him. David took refuge with the prophet Samuel in Naioth (a word meaning *dwelling*, and possibly indicating a college of prophets).

When Saul's messengers and Saul himself came, they saw the prophets prophesying with Samuel at their head. Again the Spirit came upon King Saul and he also prophesied, stripping off his clothes and lying naked on the ground as a psychological reaction of repentance (1 Samuel 10:5-13; 19:18-24).

Some scholars regard these sons of the prophets as raving dervishes. It is true that hard-bitten soldiers refer to one of them as 'this maniac' or 'madman' (2 Kings 9:11), but we have already seen that prophets appeared to be taken out of themselves when inspiration came upon them. There is no reason to suppose that these earlier prophets had a different message from the later written prophets. Their task was to exalt the God of Israel and to contend with those, including false prophets, who were turning away to the gods of Canaan.

The gods of Canaan certainly had their own prophets, and when Queen Jezebel surrounded herself with some 850 of them at her court (1 Kings 18:19), Elijah became the great champion of the true God against the prophets and supporters of the Phoenician Baal.

In the northern kingdom of Israel there were also some 400 other prophetic hangers-on at court, and the story in 1 Kings 22 shows an interesting facet of God's inspiration. King Jehoshaphat of Judah was asked by King Ahab of Israel to join him on a campaign to re-take Ramoth-gilead. A number of prophets declared that the Lord would give them the city. Jehoshaphat was suspicious and asked for another prophet.

Micaiah was sent for, and was warned of what the others had said. So in a sarcastic voice he repeated the words of the other prophets, 'Attack and be victorious, for the LORD will give it into the King's hand' (1 Kings 22:15 NIV). It was obvious that this was sarcasm, and he finally declared that in a vision he had seen Israel's army scattered. He went further, and described another vision where the Lord is on his throne and asks who among the host of heaven would entice King Ahab to go to his death at Ramoth-gilead. Eventually one spirit agrees to do it, and to 'be a deceiving spirit in the mouths of all his prophets' (verse 23). The Lord sent him to do this.

The interesting thing about this story is that God did not compel Ahab to go to his death. He gave him the choice by inspiring Micaiah, as well as allowing a spirit to sway the false prophets. It is clear from the story that Ahab chose the voices that told him to do what he wanted to do anyway.

20: Hypnosis

Prophecy in general came to an end in ancient Israel in about 400 BC. It reappeared again with the coming of Jesus. Luke records in his Gospel the prophecy of Zechariah concerning his son, John the Baptist (Luke 1:67). The book of Acts mentions Christian prophets several times, including one who foretold a coming famine (Acts 11:27-30), and 'Judas and Silas, who themselves were prophets, said much to encourage and strengthen the believers' (Acts 15:32 NIV).

At Corinth, prophets spoke in the Christian congregations, and although the apostle Paul recognised their inspiration he also recognised that they could control the prophetic outburst from their spirits when this made for better order in the congregation (1 Corinthians 14:29-33). The important place of the prophets is shown by the statement that the church is 'built on the foundation of the apostles and prophets' (Ephesians 2:20).

Prophecy died out after a time, as it had in the Jewish

church. We can see a possible reason. Jewish prophecy ceased when the Old Testament was completed; Christian prophecy ceased when the New Testament was completed and generally available. So long as the books of the New Testament were few and far between, and the apostles scattered, there was need of inspired prophets to teach the new truths of God in Christ. Local Christians were not left to find their own ideas of the meaning of the Christian faith.

As in Old Testament times, there were false prophets who had to be tested by their attitude to the basic facts of the incarnation, which converts had been taught when they became Christians. John writes emphatically that prophets who denied the incarnation were inspired by a spirit which was anti-God and anti-Christ (1 John 4:1-3).

Prophets were unique people; the agents of God's direct inspiration. Essentially they were men to whom God spoke in a direct way. The prophets' manner of speaking under inspiration differed from that of ordinary people, but what came via a deep level could be expressed in an intelligent way. The messages could be written down, and those universal values are preserved in our Old Testament.

Could the prophets remember what they had said or seen when they were inspired? As an extreme instance can we believe that Jeremiah could dictate to his scribe in 605 BC all the prophecies he had pronounced since 626 BC (Jeremiah 36:1-4)?

Hypnosis has shown the extraordinary retentiveness of memories in the unconscious. A subject under hypnosis by Dr Harold Rosen in Toronto produced a strange script which turned out to be in an extinct language.

Under hypnosis one man began speaking in Oscan, a language spoken in Italy in the third century BC. He was even able to write down an Oscan curse. Only later, during additional sessions of hypnosis, was it discovered that the man had recently looked at an Oscan grammar in the library. Several phrases had registered in his unconscious mind and found expression in the hypnotic state. (*A Scientific Report on the Search for Bridey Murphy.* Harold Rosen et al, Julian Press, 1956.)

This example throws light on many of the claims to remember under hypnosis events in some previous incarnation. More and more of these 'proofs' of reincarnation have been traced back to books and childhood stories, long since forgotten, but reproduced as historical memories.

Naturally, God did not need the help of a hypnotist to draw out Jeremiah's memory of what he had said in the past; God himself drew out the memories directly. Maybe some of the Gospel records were drawn out in the same way, and then the various stories and teachings almost immediately fell into a form which was taught verbatim on every occasion. The content of John's Gospel was drawn from John's buried memories, and John records Christ's promise that the Holy Spirit 'will remind you of everything I have said to you' (John 14:26 NIV). So, once again, God uses human inner resources to accomplish his purposes.

There are two biblical records of an induced hypnotic state which I do not think have been noticed. In Genesis chapter 19 the men of Sodom are said to be 'struck with blindness' by the angels, so that they cannot find the door to Lot's house. This suggestion of invisibility of people or things is a standard demonstration in hypnosis. The subject cannot see people and objects that are actually there.

In 2 Kings 6, in answer to the prophet Elisha's prayer, God strikes the invaders with blindness, so that Elisha tells them that they have come to the wrong city and leads them into the heart of enemy territory. The Hebrew word *sanverim* is used on these two occasions only, and is translated as 'blindness'. Both these stories appeared strange to me until I realised that God was using the same suggestible centre as that reached by hypnotists.

Hypnotism, as we have seen, has demonstrated the possible recall of buried memories from the whole of life. This is relevant for the record of the opening of the books at the Judgment. 'And I saw the dead, great and small, standing before the throne, and books were opened. Another book was opened, which is the book of life. The dead were judged according to what they had done as recorded in the books' (Revelation 20:12). We should not picture ourselves as queuing at some heavenly library waiting for our book. Our own total memories constitute the books that will be opened on that day.

For reference:
Ian Wilson: *Mind out of Time* (Gollanz, 1981). This is one of several books which expose some claims of memories of previous lives produced under hypnotism.

21: Spells and Witchcraft

I believe the only example of spells in the Bible occurs in the book of Ezekiel. 'Woe to the women who sew magic charms on all their wrists and make veils of various lengths for their heads in order to ensnare people' (Ezekiel 13:17-23 NIV). What these women were doing must have been clear to Ezekiel's contemporaries, but is far from clear to us now.

They evidently accepted payment to put death spells on some people, and to give guarantees of safety to others. For this, they used magic wristbands and veils. Possibly someone who wanted to put a curse on another person would get hold of hair or blood from the intended victim and wear it in a band on which a curse had been laid.

Is there any modern counterpart to such practices? Taking spells first, witches, witchdoctors and magicians are familiar with curses that can be laid through the possession of an object belonging to the victim. It seems that we are somehow linked to what has once belonged to us.

The majority of deaths that result from such curses are almost certainly due to auto-suggestion, since the victim is made aware of the curse by signs left on his doorstep. Similarly, an amateur palmist at a local Bingo club told another member that he could not see any future for him in his hand. The man was dead in a fortnight, and I should judge it to be more than a fifty percent chance that his death was due to auto-suggestion.

Where a curse is put on someone, there may well be a direct psychic force in addition to the force of suggestion. Certainly, missionaries have been aware of an unseen black force that has confronted them when the local witch doctor has mobilized his powers against the gospel work. CT Studd [1860-1931] once found himself unable to speak at a gathering in Africa, until by an effort he broke through in the name of Christ. The witch doctors had gathered to silence him.

In his book, *Experiences of a Present Day Exorcist* (Wm Kimber, 1970), Donald Omand gives two stories from his personal experience of occasions when little figures were plaited from straw to represent someone on whom a curse was to be placed. As the figure was pierced with pins, so the victim was taken ill. One case was probably due to suggestion, but in the other instance, where a healthy young Nazi died suddenly of angina, the victim had no knowledge of the figure that was hidden in his room with a pin buried in its 'heart'.

There is another form of witchcraft today which has had some publicity on TV and radio. There have been interviews with women who claim to be heads of covens or groups of witches. The late curator of the Isle of Man folk museum, Gerald Gardner [1884-1964], wrote a book, *Witchcraft Today* (Rider, 1954), in which he claimed to be the head of a coven. He disowned all connection with

Satanism, and such description as he was free to give of this form of witchcraft [Wicca] showed that it was a form of Nature worship, totally pagan, centring in a goddess like the Babylonian Ishtar. Again there is the manipulation of psychic force, and the coven, naked and oiled, join in a circle to generate power which they then try to project for beneficial purposes.

To return to the other type of witchcraft, which crosses the border into black magic, this is often an occasion for every kind of sexual orgy. From time to time the papers print revelations which may be exaggerated, but which I am sure are basically true. Sometimes there is defiant Satanism.

A Christian has the assurance from the Bible that God is ultimately in control, however much God allows freedom to Satan and to human beings. Jesus Christ has made the victory sure, as we saw in an earlier chapter. If one does not accept the Bible, one can gamble on the hypothesis that the God of the Christians is not as strong as he professes to be, and that with enough supporters Satan will eventually triumph. Looked at through purely human eyes there is much in the world situation to support this.

Thus people turn to Satanism, and challenge God by desecrating objects that are used in Christian worship such as the Communion bread (or wafer) and wine, and vestments and candles from churches. Parodies of Christian services and prayers are part and parcel of the ceremonies. Churchyards are desecrated, and occasionally there are suspected ritual murders.

One doubts whether the majority of these gatherings generate much psychic force, but undoubtedly they form channels for the liberation of evil atmospheres into the world of today. There is, however, a further world of straight magic. The Bible recognizes Egyptian magicians who produced comparable phenomena to what God produced through Moses and Aaron, though only up to a point (Exodus 7:10-12,22; 8:7,18).

The most notorious of modern magicians was Aleister Crowley [1875-1947]. His books are still being sold, but his moral behaviour and his defiance of God are appalling by any standards.

There are, however, other non-Christian magicians who regard moral strictness as necessary for their success. Indeed, their pattern of development comes close to some forms of mysticism, as AD Duncan points out in *The Christ, Psychotherapy, and Magic* (Allen & Unwin, 1969), the difference being that 'The mystic seeks God. The magician seeks the things of God' (page 50).

We postulate, then, a realm and activity of psychic force whereby, without introducing the intervention of spirit beings, some people can project an invisible influence beyond the reach of their physical senses.

Then why should everyone not train himself to manipulate and be immersed in these energies? The answer seems to me to be a practical one. Those who cultivate them tend to become either bad, like black magicians, or power-inflated like other magicians and witches, or pantheistic or atheistic like practitioners of some forms of yoga who explore the personal and impersonal inner world without looking to God above.

If God wishes to use any man's latent psychic force, he will naturally do so. We only run into trouble when we try to manipulate it for ourselves. A few Christian mystics, for instance, have experienced strange physical phenomena such as levitation, but these have been incidental and not sought in themselves. Cases are included in Father Herbert Thurston's two books, *The Physical Phenomena of Mysticism* (Burns Oates, 1952) and *Surprising Mystics* (Burns Oates, 1955).

We need not be afraid of meditation if it is properly directed. In fact, it should form part of a daily time of personal Bible reading and prayer. Its misuse is to allow the mind to go passive and accept whatever comes up from the depths, as with an LSD trip.

Christian meditation is anchored to what God has revealed in Scripture. Meditation might, for example, be on Christ as the Bread of life, the Water of life, or the Way; or it might soak in a verse from the daily Scripture portion. Generally, we relate our meditation to union with God.

Where Christians differ from say eastern mystics is that we do not meditate on union with an unknown immanent god, but on a God who is known in and through Jesus Christ and his death on the cross, and in the indwelling of the Holy Spirit.

The heart of the matter is summed up in Ephesians 2:18, 'Through Jesus Christ we have access in one Spirit to the Father'. Whatever techniques we use for quietening our mind and body, we aim at allowing the words of Scripture to come to life in our inner being, so that they can be translated into dynamic life.

22: Tea-leaves

Psychometry is the term for taking an object and becoming aware of its owner, often including his or her past, present and future. Dr Eugene Osty [1874-1938] made a special study of this ability, a documented it in his book *Super-normal Faculties in Man*, translated from the French in 1923 (Methuen). It is as though something which has been in contact with us retains a memory of us which can be read by others. Possibly this is more than a memory; it may be a representative of us as we are, and so we may be cursed and maltreated through it. On the other hand, it may be a link which can be used to help us.

Such a belief underlies machines like the so-called Black Box or the Drown Machine*, and Radionics. The practitioner takes a blood spot and uses it to diagnose the

---

* A quick internet search will give more information on these machines from many sources, although with varying levels of reliability. Dr Ruth B Drown was arrested (rightly or wrongly, depending on your viewpoint) by the California State Department of Public Health in 1963 for her claims concerning the Drown machine, but died in 1965 while awaiting trial. Two of her colleagues were found guilty of grand theft for their part in the operation.

illness of the person who supplied the blood, and can then [claim to] treat the spot as though it was the actual patient.

The nearest parallel to this in the Bible is the taking of handkerchiefs and work aprons which had been in contact with the apostle Paul's skin. (The word 'skin', as in the NEB, is the accurate translation, rather than 'body'.) These objects were taken to people who were ill or possessed, with the result that they were cured, just as Paul himself was used to cure illnesses (Acts 19:11-12). These were not in fact blessed handkerchiefs, like those we occasionally read about today, but cloths and aprons which Paul used in his work as a tentmaker. In this connection we also remember the incident where a woman with a haemorrhage touched the fringe of Christ's garment and was healed (Matthew 9:20-22).

It gives us pause for thought that objects which have been in contact with us are somehow imprinted by us. This phenomenon probably accounts for the happy, sad or frightening atmospheres in different houses. Some people are more sensitive to such atmospheres than others.

One lady tells how she went into an empty room and felt so battered emotionally that she had to run out. Later, she discovered that two people had recently quarrelled violently in the room. There is a strange passage in the book of Leviticus which says that, through the sins of the Canaanites, 'the land was defiled ... and vomited out its inhabitants' (Leviticus 18:24-25 NIV). This defilement was something that all too easily overwhelmed the Israelites when they came into the land.

It is possible that moral contamination is sometimes contagious, and creates an atmosphere of infection. Crazes such as drug abuse and solvent abuse are obviously copied, but the more victims there are, the more the influence spreads through the pervading atmosphere.

Buildings where Christians meet for worship absorb their own atmosphere. Some worshippers do not seem to sense this, but generally there is a calming atmosphere in an old church which is conducive to reverence before God. On the other hand, some churches are restless.

We cannot rule out the power of relics and holy places. When some object or place has been the focus of devotion for generations, irrespective of its original genuineness, it accumulates an attractive power that radiates to increasing numbers of people. That is why Lourdes and Fatima are a focus of blessing to many, even though we may not believe the theology behind them.

Many Christians make pilgrimages to places hallowed by generations of Christians, such as Glastonbury and Iona, and Keswick with its Christian convention meetings emphasizing that members of all denominations are 'one in Christ Jesus'.

As we have seen, objects belonging to someone can be taken and used for harm, to put a curse on the owner.

Another form of unseen influence involves what is loosely called fortune-telling. Fortune-tellers may use various methods such as cards, tea-leaves and crystal balls to discover the future of their clients. Whatever the method, probably some degree of clairvoyance is involved. Clairvoyance can transcend time as we have seen, and a fortune-teller may enter in some way into the client's prospects.

Eugene Osty, the French investigator, visited a number of people, both spiritualists and non-spiritualists, who claimed to have the faculty of precognition, asking them for details of his own immediate and more remote future. He also took with him objects belonging to friends of his, and asked for descriptions of the past, present and future of their owners.

Osty concluded, 'Twelve years of personal experiment, with many metagnomic* percipients and a considerable number of persons, have given me absolute certainty that there are human beings who can foretell the future of other persons. I say *the future of other persons*, I do not say *the future in general,* which I have not verified personally' (*Supernatural Faculties in Man,* Methuen, 1923, page 110).

This is an important proviso. Foretelling generally refers to the subject's personal future experience, and sees the future as the subject will experience it. For example, Osty says, 'No metagnomic subject seems to have foreseen the war [World War I] as a collective fact ... and when it had begun, none were found to give information on its successive phases' (page 178). On the other hand, true descriptions were given of the personal war experiences of Osty and others.

None of Osty's subjects, so far as I can see, made use of objects such as cards or tea-leaves. But if they had done, I have no doubt that their messages would have come from the same source, namely clairvoyance. Certainly a crystal ball and the surface of a shining liquid can release a capacity to see pictures of the future of a client. The pictures come from the inner mind, but are projected onto the ball or the liquid.

In Deuteronomy 18:10-11 God specifically forbids fortune-telling. The realm of future events, like the realm of

---

* Metagnomic – information obtained by means other than reason or the five senses.

113

the return of the spirits after death, belongs to God. However, God disclosed certain future crises in the Bible, and from time to time I believe he shows us, or grants us intuition of, some coming event in our own lives. This may simply come to us through some experience or situation, and become meaningful when later we encounter the someone or the something else for which God was preparing us. The first experience has been a divine preparation for the second. This, however, is different from our deliberately peering into the future.

23: Consulting the Cards

Nowhere in the Bible does God tell anyone to make life easier by finding out beforehand what is going to happen, although there are many occasions when it would be helpful to know.

We can only speculate on the reasons for this silence about the future. Knowledge of the future tends to nurture a passive attitude to life. We would quickly become optimistic or pessimistic in the light of what we discovered about the future. An impending fortune makes us careless with money today; the threat of an accident keeps us on edge for weeks. The book of Ecclesiastes, among its many wise thoughts, teaches that men and women must face an unseen future by trusting God who alone knows.

Trust in fortune-telling also tends to underrate the use of intelligence. A non-Christian student told me of his disgust at the behaviour of some of his fellow students who would repeatedly lay out the cards to tell them what to do, instead of using their native commonsense.

God does not intend us to have absolute certainty about the future, but lacking foreknowledge, to use our commonsense. When we ask for God's guidance, this has to take account of our being in an uncertain world situation; God will not necessarily alter the situation to suit our convenience.

A third reason for rejecting fortune-telling is that it involves a feeling of pulling away from God. The fortune-teller puts himself into a semi-divine position, giving his clients the impression that they can turn to him to discover what God would otherwise conceal from them. Admittedly, in other spheres we do not belittle God if we turn to an expert for help. When the drain is blocked we call in the plumber. Nonetheless, I believe that most Christians feel there is a difference in consulting a fortune-teller. Habitual dependence on fortune-telling is bound to decrease trust in God.

Two ancient methods of guidance have become popular again today: the Tarot and the I Ching. The Tarot cards date back certainly to the early 1400s AD, and probably many centuries earlier. A pack of Tarot cards consists of fifty-six cards of four suits, described as Wands, Cups, Swords and Pentacles. In addition, there is a further set of twenty-two Major Arcana cards, each with a distinctive picture such as The Emperor, The Empress, High Priest, Temperance, The Devil, Sun, Moon, Judgment, The Hanged Man and The Fool. Pictures differ from pack to pack according to the artist, but the symbols are always the same.

In a consultation, the cards are shuffled and laid out, and readings are made from their position in relation to each other. An expert can interpret them for a client, or one can learn to interpret them for oneself. Some people refuse to take any important decision without consulting the Tarot cards. On the other hand some people reject the use of the Tarot cards for fortune-telling, but use them for meditation on the inner illumination of the relations between God, man and life.

The I Ching, whose 'bible' has been translated from Chinese into English in three versions, has been used for divination since before the time of Confucius [c. 500 BC], and was required study for some two thousand years for candidates entering the Chinese Imperial Civil Service. It cannot therefore be easily dismissed, especially since it was commended by the psychologist CG Jung.

By the manipulation of the dried stalks of a yarrow plant, or by the tossing or throwing of coins, a person looks for the answer to a particular question. The position of the stalks, or fall of the coins, indicates a particular hexagram or hexagrams in the book. There are sixty-four hexagrams, each giving an answer on each of its six lines, and on the total, making seven possible answers in all. Thus [in this example] there are 448 possible answers. The words on the line include: 'Integrity', 'Righteous persistence brings rewards', 'Not favourable to go forward yet', and similar answers. The book contains commentaries on each of them.

The I Ching differs from other fortune-telling methods. It does not forecast the future, but says what the person consulting it ought to do if he or she is to be in harmony with the flow of the universe.

Carl Jung describes how he spent hours testing the I Ching, and concludes, 'All sorts of undeniably remarkable results emerged – meaningful connections with my own thought processes which I could not explain to myself.'

Jung tried to explain the phenomenon by the word synchronicity, which has come to be especially associated with him. The word means 'meaningful coincidence', and Jung and others have tried to account for it.

This is a useful point at which to discuss coincidence. Lately I have puzzled over several incredible coincidences which have happened to me. Not long ago I was preparing a sermon on the subject of grace. As it is a subject on which one can easily say something misleading, I decided to write out the whole sermon beforehand. I was about to quote the fact that some parents have named their children Grace, and that a friend of mine called his daughter Charis, the Greek word for grace. I had not seen Charis, the girl in question, for probably thirty years, but at that moment the phone rang; it was Charis herself, asking me to do something.

Again, take this incident of my grandfather's gold watch which we planned to give to our grandson who lives in Sydney, Australia. But how could we send it safely to him for his coming-of-age? I was invited to take a weekday service at a Bristol church to which I had been just two or three times previously. After the service two visitors appeared, to look round the historic building. You can guess the rest: they were from Sydney, and were returning there in ten days' time. So our grandson got the watch safely.

Incidents like this which happen to all kinds of people are acausal. Our days are filled with causes and effects. Things happen in sequence through our planning, or through anticipated events. But suddenly something occurs entirely unplanned, and yet with a definite relation to our state, though uncaused. My being asked to take the service, and the visitors deciding to visit that church at that time, came together uncaused, yet as though the situation had been planned. Synchronicity is not pure chance, but 'a causal explanation of these phenomena is not even thinkable in intellectual terms' (Jung).

Jung naturally brings in the unconscious, which as we have seen represents a field of the mind which has a deeper awareness than consciousness, and somehow moves outside space and time. I think Jung is saying that in the I Ching the unconscious perceives the right answer to the question: 'What shall I do?' The fall of the stalks 'happens' to coincide with this one out of many possible answers in the hexagrams.

But in the two examples that I quoted from my own recent experience, one may assume the working of an attracting telepathy which operated unknown to Charis, the two visitors or myself. But who telepathised whom? Synchronicity may be planned by God as a means of guidance. When an earthquake blocked the River Jordan at the gorge near the town of Adam at the very moment when the Israelites needed to cross the river, God's synchronicity was at work (Joshua 3).

Without realising it, Joshua was led to the edge of the Jordan at the exact moment when the water was reduced to a trickle. The same natural event has happened at the same place several times since, but without the same significance. Again, when God told Gideon to go by night to the camp of the enemy, he arrived at the exact moment when a soldier was telling a significant dream (Judges 7:9-14).

When we put the day into God's hands, should we notice more acausal, or God-caused, happenings than we do? If the I Ching merely interprets myself in showing what I ought to do, why should not a Christian use it? I have to fall back on the unscientific feeling that I confessed previously. It does not feel right, and it does not intensify my love for Jesus Christ, being based as it is on a non-Christian philosophy which has little place for the personal Creator.

It is very relevant that at the city of Ephesus a number of new converts to Christianity who 'had practised sorcery, brought their scrolls together and burned them publicly' (Acts 19:19 NIV).

Some people believe that the Bible *encourages* magic and superstitious practices. Some want to include even the drawing of lots as divination – but this is absurd. Lots were used to secure fair treatment in distributing the Promised Land among the tribes of Israel, and to choose Saul as first king of Israel.

The last recorded use of the lot in the Bible was in the choice of Matthias as the new apostle to replace Judas (Acts 1:23-26), which as some have pointed out was before the pouring out of the guiding Spirit at Pentecost. After that, it was the Holy Spirit who said, 'Set apart for me Barnabas and Saul ...' (Acts 13:2).

The Urim and the Thummin seem to represent another form of lot. They were worn on the breastplate of the High Priest (Exodus 28:30), and were used on occasion to give a Yes/No answer. David was given Yes answers to two questions he put concerning his possible arrest (1 Samuel 23:9-12). On another occasion, King Saul said, 'If this guilt is in me or in Jonathan ... give Urim; but if in Israel, give Thummin' (1 Samuel 14:41 NIV). This is the nearest we come to discovering how the two stones were used, but we notice that they were used solemnly, in the context of prayer. Possibly the stones were drawn out of their pouch containers.

An interesting piece of occult practice was the use of the *teraphim* (variously translated, e.g. *household gods*, *idols*). This was evidently an image, sometimes small enough to be concealed easily, as by Rachel who stole her father Laban's teraphim (Genesis 31:34). Yet the image could also be quite large, since King David's wife put the teraphim in his bed to deceive the messengers of Saul into thinking he had been taken ill (1 Samuel 19:13). Elsewhere, teraphim are used for magical purposes. In Zechariah 10:2 teraphim are grouped with diviners as giving lying utterances.

Probably the best way of bringing these passages together is to derive the word *teraphim* from the Hebrew *rephaim,* meaning the dead, or the shades. They may have been images of departed ancestors, preserved for a similar purpose to the Chinese ancestral tablets. Records from Mesopotamia show that possession of the household idols gave a son or son-in-law the primal right of inheritance. This would explain Rachel's theft in the interest of her husband Joseph.

Did Joseph practise hydromancy [water divination] in Egypt? His steward said that the cup in Benjamin's sack was the one by which Joseph divined (Genesis 44:5), the reference being to a practice known as scrying. By gazing fixedly into a liquid, a psychically inclined person sees pictures taking shape, as in crystal gazing. The probability is that light auto-hypnotism releases psychic vision. We cannot be certain that Joseph actually used this method, since it comes as part of a deliberately deceiving series of incidents to fool his brothers.

Elsewhere in the New Testament there are accounts of two magicians. One is Simon, who after an apparent conversion tried to bribe Peter and John to give him power to confer the Holy Spirit (Acts 8:9-24). As Simon Magus, he became notorious as both a magician and as founder of a strange heresy. The other magician mentioned in the New Testament is Elymas, a Jew on Cyprus, who resisted Paul and Barnabas and was struck blind (Acts 13:6-11). Both are described by the Greek word *magos*.

24: Messages From Beyond

One other natural capacity ought to be mentioned in more detail before looking again at the Ouija board. This goes by the name of *cryptomnesia*, or latent memory, such as the Oscan memories on pages 102-3. Many things that we have completely forgotten can be recalled under hypnotism. Moreover, items that we are not aware of having seen can be stored in our memories. Thus, there has been considerable discussion on the morality of subliminal advertising, since tests have shown that a slogan flashed during a programme on the TV or cinema screen for too brief a period to register on the conscious mind, has penetrated sufficiently to create a response via the deeper part of the mind.

Could this factor have a bearing on the messages given at some seances? The names and addresses of two people who had recently died may well have come from cryptomnesia if a member of the group had noticed the announcement in the paper. A case in point took place in the nineteenth century when Stainton Moses [1839-1892], to whom we have already referred [page 44], received a communication purporting to come from a certain Abraham Florentine who had fought in the American war of 1812, and who had died at Brooklyn on August 5th 1874, aged 83 years, 1 month and 17 days. These details were correct, except that his actual age had been 83 years, 1 month and 27 days, as his widow testified.

This may seem like an unimportant accidental slip in a single figure, but this same slip had already been made in Florentine's obituary notices in two American papers. It is therefore likely that Stainton Moses had in fact seen a copy of one of the papers, although the obituary notice had not registered on his conscious mind.

There may be another explanation too, for the mysterious Peter Rooney ['from Boston' who 'said' in the school cellar that he had committed suicide ten days previously by throwing himself under a tram – see page 25]. He may have been a creation from the inspirational depths of someone's mind, who was forthwith adopted by the subconscious of the group as a real character.

The cellar where the boys held their seance was admittedly a place of bad repute, and they were likely to pick up something – not necessarily someone – from the past, a picture drawn from the imaginative depths of the boys' minds. One could go further, and on the lines of the experiments in psychometry say that some evil happenings had been imprinted on the surroundings and were picked up by the released faculties of the boys.

This theory of imprinting is a perfectly good hypothesis to account for some hauntings. Generally a haunting centres in a person or people who had passed through some highly emotional experience, such as murder or torture, or who had been emotionally attached to a house.

We need not suppose that they return personally in order to be murdered once again, but rather that some people who can tune in to the right 'wave' perceive the person or event over again.

In his autobiography, *Behind the Brass Plate* (Sampson Low, 1928), Dr AT Schofield relates how he went to a country house accompanied by a Christian lady who had second sight. While they were sitting in the hall this lady suddenly jumped up and called to him to stop two men whom she saw fighting violently in the further corner of the hall. Dr Schofield saw nothing, but when the hostess appeared she took it all quite calmly and said that others had seen the same thing. The two men were a father and son who had lived some 200 years before.

Sometimes I am asked for Scriptural evidence for this theory of imprinting as an explanation of haunting. It is impossible to produce any, since Scripture never mentions haunting. All that we can do, therefore, when we encounter what seems to be a haunting, whether harmless, or violent as with poltergeists, is to produce a hypothesis that makes sense and that does not run counter to Scripture in other respects.

So if we say that imprinting accounts for some hauntings, we have a sensible theory. Probably one sees the event as one would have seen it from the same approximate position when it happened, but it is possible that such temporary second sight builds on the 'picture', and actually produces in us the emotions of the participants, as happens with psychometry.

Occasionally imprinting is picked up during the lifetime of the original participants. In his book, *Exorcising Devils* (Hale, 1976), Dom Robert Petitpierre tells of a lady gifted with second sight who went to stay with a family she had not previously met. As she came downstairs to dinner the clock struck seven, and she saw a bearded man come in at the front door, while from one of the downstairs rooms a group of children ran out and flung themselves into his arms. Next moment all had vanished.

It turned out that what she had seen was the father, no longer alive, as he used to come home when his children were young, and the scene which commonly took place every evening at seven. The significance of the story is that although their father was dead, all or most of the children were still alive as grown men and women.

In the case of the boys holding a seance in the school cellar [page 25], there may well have been a man named Mercer who murdered a woman in the cellar [in 1854], but we need not suppose that she had returned from the dead to speak through the Ouija board.

The Hugh Lane communicator [allegedly from the *Lusitania*, page 24] is slightly different. Evidence is undeniable that round about the time of death, as well as during illness or at some crisis, a person has appeared or spoken to some relative or friend at a distance. One accepts the fact, but is puzzled by the mechanism involved. To take the illustration we started with on page 1, it is all very well to say that my friend actually appeared to me at the moment of his death, but in fact it was not only my friend that appeared, but the clothes which he or she was wearing at the time, or the clothes to which I was accustomed. If the spirit was there in person, were his clothes also brought in spirit form?

The standard work on this subject is GNM Tyrell's *Apparitions* (Duckworth, 1942). Out of the various possibilities, the most sensible seems to me to be basically telepathy: I become aware through mind-to-mind contact at a deep level of my friend's distress. This may remain as no more than a general uneasiness, but alternatively my conscious mind may clothe the awareness in a form or voice that becomes perceptible as a person in space.

This is sensible if we consider the phenomenon of hypnotism and post-hypnotic suggestion. Hypnotism has been grossly misused as a stunt. It is used far less nowadays, even in psychiatry. But if I were to hypnotize you, and you were a good subject, I might suggest to you that at three o'clock you would see your local Member of Parliament entering the room and sitting down in the chair next to you to talk to you about local reforms. Then at precisely three o'clock anyone else in the room would find you behaving as though all were happening as I had suggested. The MP would evidently appear to you, sit down and talk to you.

Nobody understands how hypnotism works, but it is as if I implanted an idea in the depths of your mind, and your brain then fed it back in a reverse direction. Instead of the nerve impulses from exterior sense organs stimulating certain parts of the brain to produce sight and sound, these parts of the brain are stimulated from within, so as to create the illusion that there really is a figure and a voice in the room. Incidentally, we call this figure a hallucination.

To go back to the ghost, this also is a hallucination, but it may nevertheless be what is called a veridical [truth-conveying] hallucination if it coincides with some true situation or communication that the distant person is trying to create for you.

To return to Barrett's account at the time of the sinking

of the *Lusitania* [page 24], if one or more of the group had received the telepathic awareness of the death of their friend Hugh Lane, the knowledge would emerge via the board. But, as we have seen, the fact that the communicator could not give information in later contact about a codicil to his will which was in dispute, makes one suspect that the real Hugh Lane was not present.

We note one point which Barrett does not raise at the time in his tests of the Ouija board and the jumbled letters (page 24). The sitters were blindfolded. So let us ask a realistic question. Where were the *spirit's* eyes? From the description it would sound as though they were on the pointer of the moving board. This of course is absurd. If on the other hand the spirit was aware of what was going on in the room, it would have been aware of the order of the letters, without having to go round and inspect each one – unless spirits are short-sighted.

If, however, we ask how did Sir William Barrett know what the board did, and how did the blindfolded sitters know what words it spelt out, the answer must be that there was a person who was not blindfolded and who was recording the movements of the board. If there was a spirit it must have used his eyes to locate the letters. But once the recorder knew the order of the letters, he could become the channel of the telepathic faculties of the group as a whole, and we need not postulate a spirit at all.

If group telepathy is all that is involved in the Ouija board and the tumbler, it may sound very harmless. Before we discuss the dangers, we ought to look at the possibility that spirits are actually involved, remembering as we said earlier that it may not be an *either/or* but a *both/and*.

There are some lifelong investigators of spiritualistic

phenomena who are convinced that all can be explained by fraud, or by telepathy and clairvoyance. If in place of *all*, one puts *much*, this I believe is a fair estimate.

The average person who goes to a seance jumps a logical gap when he is told something that only he and the departed relative know, or is reminded of something that he did that morning before coming to the seance. Or when he is told of some future event which does in fact come to pass, he concludes that these revelations are a proof that it is indeed his relative who has communicated.

Yet the first two pieces of information are already available for mind-to-mind telepathy – his mind and the medium's. For the third, he assumes that only a spirit can know the future. Spirits may or may not know the future, but it is certainly a fact, as Osty and others have demonstrated, that some human beings with the gift of second sight make unaided the same sort of prediction as the alleged spirit does.

25: Where Do the Departed Go?

There are various attempts to probe the mystery of death, apart from the Bible. The simplest solution is to say that there is no mystery at all. Man is no more than a material being, and when the material body dies that is the end. But if experiences such as telepathy show that a person can 'travel' beyond the range of the material senses of the body, why should not the 'traveller' continue after the body with its material senses has died.

More philosophically, we can argue from the preservation of the values that have been built up during a lifetime on earth. It is true that many things are not worth preserving, but surely the total destruction of a good man makes no sense in a world that has been working for the survival of what is best.

A more tangible proof would be if someone had returned from the hereafter. There are widows and widowers who are emphatic that their husband or wife has appeared to them after death. But if this is our only proof, it proves too much. Those who appear are always wearing the clothes they wore in their lifetime. If these appearances prove the survival of the person, they also seem to prove the survival of fabrics!

Spiritualists are not content to argue from such spontaneous appearances, but attempt to make contact with the departed through mediums or sensitives. As we have seen, even if we accept the capacity for clairvoyance, a clairvoyant medium can be picking up the thoughts, pictures and affections of the client who seeks comfort, and in good faith gives them back as though they are personal communications from the one who has passed on.

Outside of popular spiritualism there are serious investigators who are not merely concerned with finding links with individual relatives and friends who have passed on, but who investigate the total evidence. The Society for Psychical Research was formed [in 1882] to do precisely this, but after over a century, and hundreds of investigations published in their periodicals, as we have seen, members are honestly divided over the results. Do they or do they not provide adequate proof of survival?

There is one more point which is significant for me personally. There are two beliefs about which I am utterly convinced, on grounds other than the Bible, and I cannot see any way that I could ever be brought to reject either of them. One is the existence of God, and the other is my own survival.

I shall be intensely surprised if, after death, I find myself non-existent! I cannot say whether these feelings were imprinted on me through a Christian home, or whether they are, as it were, an instinctive realisation. But I am inclined to think the latter, since my Christian home would have imprinted a more definitely doctrinal belief, and these convictions seem to come from within. These two beliefs may well be residual marks of human creation in the image of God, of which Genesis speaks, although they come out more strongly in some people than in others.

One of the most remarkable *non sequiturs* of spiritualism, even of spiritualism held by members of the Christian churches, is that there is no universal Day of Judgment and no resurrection of the body. It is said that all spirits are judged at death, and have a soul-body and spirit-body in which to express themselves.

The *non sequitur* comes from the fact that the Day of Judgment and the general resurrection are always linked to the Second Coming of Christ, according to the Bible, and Christ has not yet come. So if the spirits have actually communicated and described their experiences *up to now*, they, like us, still stand on this side of the Second Coming and cannot argue that there will be no judgment and no resurrection when this occurs!

There is a further lack of bite in the spiritualists' argument. They claim to have proved the fact of life after death through communications from the departed. Again, assuming the communications to be genuine, all that they prove is that some individuals, or some parts of them, have persisted for a time beyond the grave. In his book *The Supreme Adventure* (James Clarke, 1961) Robert Crookall asserts that as spirits go on to higher spheres they can no longer make direct communication through mediums (page 228). It would be equally possible to argue that they cease to communicate because they have disintegrated!

So we must remind ourselves that we are dealing with what is often called the intermediate state, the present state of the departed person between death and the return of

Christ. The Bible has little to say about this, but what it does say is significant. The Christian departs 'to be with Christ' (Philippians 1:23). When he is absent from the body, he is 'at home with the Lord' (2 Corinthians 5:8). This presence with the Lord is in marked contrast with the communications that come through mediums, in which God and Christ are incidentals, if they are mentioned at all.

In the Bible the word *heaven* is applied in three different ways. The first meaning is the atmosphere in which the birds fly. The Hebrew describes them as 'birds of the heaven', and the RSV naturally renders this 'birds of the air'. The second meaning for heaven is the sky with the heavenly bodies which are described as 'all the host of heaven' (for example Deuteronomy 4:19).

The third meaning for heaven is the invisible centre of God's reign. It is 'above' in the sense that it is 'away from' the earth, and so above both in Britain and Australia. It was clearly located away from the earth by our Lord when he gave us the Lord's Prayer, 'Our Father, who art in heaven … Thy will be done on earth as it is in heaven…' Although we enjoy the presence of God here through his Spirit, earth is not identified with heaven.

What then happens to us when we die? I am conscious that what I am going to write will seem rather academic to people who have lost loved ones, or who are facing terminal illness and need warm comfort. All I can say is that I hope an awareness of the Bible's answer now will be worked into the depths of our being, so that when the crisis of dying comes we may find the comfort we need – and I include myself.

In contrast to the Old Testament gloom, the Christian looks forward to light and joy. This is because of the fuller experience of God in Christ. The apostle Paul longs to 'depart and be with Christ, which better by far' (Philippians 1:23 NIV). He 'would prefer to be away from the body and at home with the Lord' (2 Corinthians 5:8 NIV). Jesus Christ himself promised his disciples, 'I am going to prepare a place for you … that you also may be where I am' (John 14:2-3 NIV).

This emphasis is what one misses in the communications that appear to come through mediums. Christ is either not in the picture at all, or not in the forefront. The New Testament clearly holds out for Christians the amazing prospect of departing to a fuller experience of Father, Son and Holy Spirit. At once, any honest Christian says, 'But I am not fit'. None of us are. But the Bible has an answer to this mystery. It may sound too easy to quote the text, 'The blood of Jesus, his Son, purifies us from every sin' (1 John 1:7), but this is the nub of the whole of the gospel. Moreover, those who are alive at his return go to be 'with the Lord forever' (1 Thessalonians 4:17), without any further necessary time of purifying.

One can well understand why earnest Christians introduced the concept of purgatory, although this eventually became a very mechanical scheme for paying off the debts due to sins. Yet there are so many sins that come through temptations in the body that it would be difficult to be truly purged from them, when one no longer has a body.

Suppose we substitute *growth* for *purging*. We come into the next life forgiven and cleansed, and are aware of the centrality of God as our very life. We know him in a new way. We meet Jesus Christ, as friend meeting friend. We realise how much more we might have grown in him in this life. We have only partially used our Master's talents that he gave us. There is much more, so much more to know of God, so much growing. In fact, since he is the eternal God, and we are and remain his creatures, we shall be growing and learning throughout eternity. We shall not be bored!

If this is the Bible's solution, as I believe, it allows for complete forgiveness and immediate reception into the presence of God. There is an interesting outline of future possibilities in 1 Corinthians 3:10-15. In this life the Christian is building a house. The only foundation is defined as Jesus Christ, but on this foundation we can build gold, silver and precious stones, or wood, hay and stubble, or, one assumes, a mixture. The result will be tested by fire. If the house survives, the owner will be rewarded. If it is burned up, the owner 'will suffer loss but yet will be saved – even though only as one escaping through the flames.'

The promise of reward reminds us of Our Lord's two parables of the Talents and the Pounds, where the servants were rewarded with responsible work according to the use that they had each made of the money that their master had entrusted to them (Matthew 25:14-30; Luke 19:11-26).

I have been writing as though all these things happen immediately after death, but some belong to the Day of Judgment. It is probable that while we experience the wonderful sense of Christ's presence at death and make some progress, real growth will only be possible after we 'all appear before the judgment seat of Christ, that each one may receive what is due to him for the things done while in the body, whether good or bad.' (2 Corinthians 5:10 NIV).

Naturally we are affected when loved ones pass over. Some of us find comfort in what is called the Communion of Saints (not the same as communication with the saints).

We are 'in Christ', and they too are 'in Christ', as members of the one body of Christ we and they are still one, although we are temporarily separated.

Some people feel the Communion of Saints is too remote and want something with a warmer feel. This is the point at which some people go to mediums in the hope of receiving a convincing message. But we have to trust God that all is well. Paul told the Thessalonians not to 'grieve like the rest of mankind, who have no hope' (1 Thessalonians 4:13). We rest on the knowledge that we and they are in Jesus Christ. He does not mean we ought not to feel grief, but that our grief should not be like the grief of those for whom death is final.

But there may be exceptions. Many have seen, heard or sensed the presence of a husband or wife who has passed on. I have only recently come to accept this and to distinguish it from spiritualism. If Moses and Elijah appeared at Christ's transfiguration (Matthew 17:3) it is not wrong to believe that God sometimes allows the departed to return for some special reason.

What is important is that such visitations should be spontaneous. The purpose of such visits may be to comfort and encourage someone who has been left behind. These comings may continue for several weeks or months before they cease. Sometimes the one who returns comes once or twice to communicate something important, as in the Chaffin Will case of 1925 [detailed on page 144].

The message that Bishop Pike records in his book, *The Other Side* (Doubleday, 1968), as coming from his son who had committed suicide, is typical: 'They talk about Jesus – a mystic, a seer. Oh, but Dad, they don't talk about him as a saviour.' One contrasts this with Revelation 5:6-14.

Geraldine Cummins was an author and playwright, and a medium involved in automatic writing. Among many writings, she produced a series of scripts in the 1920s and '30s purporting to come from FWH Myers, the founder of the Society for Psychical Research, who died in 1901.

Messages in general are either attempts to prove the survival of the alleged communicators, or a continued working out of ideas that may have been begun on earth, as in the Myers scripts.

26: Can the Departed Return?

In this chapter we want to consider the evidence for returning human spirits. What can we learn from Scripture about the life of God's people after the death of the body? It is worth noticing the contrast between the Old and New Testaments. The Bible shows that until the resurrection of Jesus Christ, the state of the departed, even the godly departed, was not a happy one. They were in Sheol, described as 'the land of gloom and shadow' (Job 10:21). It is a place of silence (Psalm 115:17), and the dead know nothing (Ecclesiastes 9:5).

God's revelation in the Old Testament would have been incomplete had he not pointed forward to the future, which we now see to be the era of the Messiah. 'God will redeem my soul from the grave (Sheol)' says the psalmist (Psalm 49:15). The link with God may seem to be broken in Sheol, as it may seem to be in the dark night of experiences on earth. But the era of the Messiah is seen as one; his resurrection opens the door of Sheol, and his Second

Coming completes the transformation of the Old Testament spirits.

If this discussion seems rather academic to us who have not passed through the Old Testament era, we may round it off with another Bible mystery. At the moment of Christ's death on the cross the curtain in the Temple, which hid the innermost sanctuary, was torn in two to indicate (as Hebrews 9:8 and 10:19,20 point out) that the way into God's immediate presence is open to all. This tearing of the curtain, recorded in Matthew 27:51, may have been due to the earthquake described in the same verse.

It is the further results of this earthquake which form the mystery. 'the earth shook, and the rocks were split; the tombs also were opened, and many bodies of the saints who had fallen asleep were raised, and coming out of the tombs after his resurrection they went into the holy city and appeared to many.' (Matthew 27:51-53 RSV).

What exactly happened? We must read the passage carefully. At the moment when Jesus died, an earthquake shattered some of the graves outside the city, and threw up, or disclosed, some of the bodies. It is not said whether they had died recently, or whether some were no more than bones. This was all that happened on the afternoon of Good Friday. The bodies, or the bones, would not have been touched during the Passover. We should remember that the bodies from the three crosses had to be buried before sundown on the Friday. The law banned anyone who was 'unclean through touching the dead body of a man' from keeping the Passover with everyone else (Numbers 9:6).

The spirits, or souls, of the dead did not appear until after Jesus had risen on Easter day. Here the actual Greek wording is clear, whereas some of the English translations are misleading. The word for 'bodies' is neuter, whereas 'saints' are masculine. The Greek participle 'coming out of the graves' is masculine, agreeing with the spirits, not the bodies, that appeared to many people in the city.

But why did the spirits come out of the tombs? There are at least two possible reasons. One is that they were recognised as having belonged in life to the bodies now in the graves. The other reason is more speculative. Once the spirits were released from Sheol, they were first drawn back to the body, or what fragments of it remained, in which they had once been.

What happened afterwards? Undoubtedly they were taken up with Christ with other Old Testament saints to the realm to which we shall go at death. It makes good sense to quote Ephesians 4:8 'When he ascended on high, he led captives in his train', that is, those who had in Old Testament times been death's captives in Sheol.

It is to this new state, realm, or place, that we now turn. As we have seen, the spiritualist's description of life after death is of something like a well-supplied holiday camp. Evidently these communicators have missed the Christian sphere, and because I judge from the lives of some of them that they were Christians, I doubt whether they themselves are communicating, especially if as often happens they now attack the Christian faith.

The Bible admits that in the intermediate state after death a human being is incomplete. A human being, as planned and created by God, is a body-being. This does not mean that the person cannot exist without a body, but without a body he is not the full human being that God created. Paul describes this state as being without clothes. In 2 Corinthians 5:1-10 he says that he is well aware that there is an eternal heavenly body awaiting him (verse 1).

He longs to be alive at the Second Coming of Christ, because then he would receive his new body at once, without passing through an intermediate period of nakedness (2 Corinthians 5:2-4). However, he takes comfort in the fact that even without the body he will be at home with the Lord (verses 6-8), and he continues to live in the realization that he will one day stand before the judgment seat of Christ (verses 9-10).

Man must once again become fully man, or death will have had the last word. The idea of bodily resurrection has its difficulties, but we may approach it like this. First, the risen body of Jesus Christ is the pattern. This is argued in 1 Corinthians 15, and it is stated specifically in Philippians 3:21 that Christ will change our bodies to be like his.

Secondly, if an essential part of man is destroyed by death, then death will have conquered, and since death is the result of original and personal sin, there will be a permanent monument to sin in the existence of maimed human beings. Thus 1 Corinthians 15:26 speaks of death as the last enemy to be destroyed – the resurrection destroys him.

A third point needs careful thinking. In this life our body is an expression of ourselves. Inner character changes outward appearance. Before conversion, a person may have a degraded look. Almost immediately afterwards his whole face and bearing change. A new directing *you*, empowered by the Holy Spirit, has used your intake of food and air to mould a new body which may well become far healthier than the old. At death, you can no longer build the body that you have left behind. But as a Christian you are not without the means of expression and joy, since you are still linked to Christ by the Holy Spirit. But you are still unclothed.

At the resurrection you will be given the capacity to draw to yourself all that is needed to express yourself in a body. On earth you were limited in the extent to which you could form your body after the pattern of Christ. Now, because of the Holy Spirit within, you form an expression of yourself that is recognizably you, but is also *you* after the likeness of Christ.

On the other hand, the person who is without Christ lacks the life link during the intermediate state. He had learnt only how to express himself in a body. Those who, like the rich man in Luke 16:19-31, have lived only to indulge the body, now are scorched with the flame of unsatisfied desire (verse 24). When the opportunity comes to express themselves once again in a body, since there is a resurrection also of the lost (John 5:29), there is no joint creative work with the Holy Spirit, but only a replica of what they were on earth.

We cannot presume to sift the wheat from the tares, nor to say how God judges those who have never been confronted with the call of Christ, but the story of the rich man and Lazarus must be very relevant when it speaks of the impassable chasm between the saved and the lost in Hades, the intermediate state (Luke 16:23,26).

Do we go to heaven when we die? Yes and no. Heaven is where Christ is, and in one sense, even on earth, we are 'in the heavenly places in Christ Jesus' (Ephesians 2:6). Whether or not we call the intermediate state Hades, with Paradise as the sphere of the saved (Luke 23:43), it is where Christ radiates his presence in a fuller way than we have known on earth (Philippians 1:23).

But there is a new heaven and a new earth to come (Revelation 21 and 22), and our new bodies will be adapted for whatever conditions these may bring. Here there will be the opportunity for wholly God-centred service in the radiating glory of the Trinity (Revelation 22:3-5).

After this necessary consideration of the present state of the departed, we come back to our original question of whether departed spirits can return. Jesus, of course, rose from the dead in bodily form. Omitting those who were temporarily restored to life again, the Bible shows that they have done so on two occasions.

The first we have already looked at, when Samuel came back when called up by the medium from Endor. This was to tell Saul that he would fall in battle next day (1 Samuel 28).

The only possible example in the New Testament which has sometimes been quoted as a seance is the transfiguration (Matthew 17:1-13; Mark 9:2-13; Luke 9:28-36). But the once-for-all experience on the top of a mountain is very different from repeated seances in darkened rooms. The disciples were *not* told to go and do likewise, which they were with other things that Jesus did.

Moses and Elijah conversed with Christ (Matthew 17:3). Allowing for the fact that Elijah did not die in the normal way (2 Kings 2:11), God deliberately planned for these two representatives of the Law and the Prophets to come back and talk with the Messiah about his coming death, which had been the theme of the Law and the Prophets (Luke 9:31 and 24:27).

These two single examples, which include no encouragement to secure their repetition, do not justify modern attempts to bring the departed back to the seance room.

There are, as we have seen, many modern cases of the spontaneous appearance of loved ones around the time of their death, without any intervention by mediums. Moreover, there is no reason why God should not for his own purposes allow a spirit to return. In the story of the rich man and Lazarus, Abraham did not say that it was *impossible* for Lazarus, the beggar, to return to earth, but that it would be useless for him to try to influence the rich man's brothers if he did return (Luke 16:27-31).

One story that always seems to me to be genuine is the Chaffin will case. James Chaffin died in North Carolina in 1921. His only known will had been made in 1905, and by it he left all his property to his third son. The will was proved, but the son died about a year after inheriting everything. In 1925 the second son had several visions of his father dressed in his old black overcoat.

On one occasion, the father said, 'You will find my will in my overcoat pocket'. The elder brother had the overcoat, but in a sewn-up inner pocket there was a paper saying, 'Read the 27th chapter of Genesis in my daddie's old Bible'.

The Bible was in a drawer, and between the pages where Genesis 27 was printed, there was another will made in 1919 by which the father divided his property equally between his four sons. [The handwriting on the will was accepted as genuine by all the family, including the widow of the son who had inherited all, even though it meant losing most of her inheritance.] This would seem to be a spontaneous communication from Chaffin himself, and no medium was involved.

There is nothing in Scripture to suggest that the departed are all around us and watching what we are doing. Samuel, Moses and Elijah had certain specific knowledge,

CHRISTIANS AND THE SUPERNATURAL

as we have seen; but all three on earth had had the gift of prophecy, which was something over and above their natural perception. It involved receiving direct communication from God. If God sent them back on a special mission, he told them what they needed to know, and there is no evidence that they picked up their knowledge from observation of what was passing on earth.

In this context, one of the most misapplied verses is Hebrews 12:1, where 'the cloud of witnesses' is interpreted as a crowd of spectators. The word witness in English has this ambiguity, but the NEB sensibly makes the meaning clear by translating, 'With all these witnesses to faith around us like a cloud', thus referring us back to chapter 11, to the examples of faithful testimony (*witness*) even to death that we must ever keep before our eyes. In fact, the Greek word for witness is identical with the English martyr.

We cannot tell then whether the departed know what we are doing, and it is unlikely that they are wandering invisibly around the world. Since Christians are 'in Christ' both in life and death, Christ forms the ground of union between us all, and as occasion arises our loved ones may be aware through him of some of the joys and sorrows through which we are passing. They may be told when someone they have loved is about to join them, for there are examples of deathbed visions when the one who is dying speaks of the presence of loved ones who have passed on.

It is natural to want to continue to pray for the departed, just as we prayed for them during their lifetime. Here we have a conflict between heart and head. There is nothing in the Bible to support prayer for the departed. Nevertheless, since the Bible does not forbid prayers for the dead, I would never be so cruel as to argue with someone who found them a comfort. The difficulty is to know what to pray for. Prayer needs faith, and faith needs to know what God has promised to give in answer to prayer.

The usual formal prayers, such as 'May the souls of the faithful rest in peace', and 'Let light perpetual shine upon them' merely assert what the faithful already enjoy, and what the early Christians knew they were enjoying and did not need to ask for. To pray for the salvation of the lost is very different, and God has not given us any assurance of faith for that.

What is certainly justified is meditative prayer, letting the realisation sink in that we are still together in the bond of love, and that they have passed into the land of joy, and live in 'the nearer presence' of the Lord. And that we shall meet them once more.

Some Christians are troubled by the thought that we might not recognise our friends in heaven, while others are worried by the thought of spending eternity with people they dislike. The atmosphere of perfect love will solve both problems. The love-tie on earth will be still greater in heaven, and will melt away the antagonisms of this life.

27: How Spirits Enter

We can begin to see reasons why the Bible clamps down absolutely on attempts to consult spirits. Either we receive what are no more than messages from our own hearts by telepathic awareness and psychometry; or if we are interested in obtaining descriptions of conditions in the next world, or religious and philosophical information, the communications turn out to be cleverly-twisted attacks on the uniqueness of the Christian revelation.

In a seance, Jesus Christ may be given the exalted position that Satan offered him in the wilderness temptations and that he refused (Matthew 4:8-11); but he is not given the supreme position that his Father gave him as the only Son, truly God, who became Man and triumphed on the cross, and in his resurrection and exaltation (Philippians 2:5-11). He is not the Christ whom John saw in heaven (Revelation 1 and 5). One must make the choice between Jesus Christ as he gives himself to us in the New Testament, and the vague teachings of the clever spirit communicators.

147

In this chapter we want to discover other possible spirit manifestations, and also see how spirits can influence us from within. A good place to begin is with poltergeists activity, a term we have mentioned in passing several times already. It is a German word meaning *noisy spirits*. In his book *Between Christ and Satan* (Evangelization Publishers, 1961) [later edition entitled *The Lure of the Occult*], Dr Kurt Koch whom we have already mentioned [page 37], has been badly served by his translator. The German *poltergeist* has been rendered *spook*, which so far as I know is never used of poltergeists, but is just a word of childish fun to describe an 'ordinary' ghost.

We have regarded some hauntings as the result of imprints. These are the hauntings where material objects are not moved, and everything after the appearance is as it was before. But poltergeists move things, and the noise that they make is usually the banging of the objects they displace.

Certainly one must eliminate some of the reported cases of poltergeists, since they have turned out to be cleverly staged frauds by children, or sometimes vibration caused by underground streams or by traffic, or rats or mice in the walls. Yet when such cases have been eliminated, it is significant that similar phenomena have been recorded independently down the centuries from all parts of the world. Hereward Carrington in *The Invisible World* (Rider, 1947) mentions his analysis of some 320 cases between AD 530 and 1935, of which he finds 278 that cannot be explained by natural laws.

Harry Price in *Poltergeist over England* (Country Life Ltd, 1945) records even more. They occur, he finds, regularly in highly civilized countries as well as in primitive communities. Very similar things happen in each case. Furniture and other household objects are moved about; crockery and stones are thrown – sometimes in slow motion or round corners. Occasionally bedclothes are pulled off and the beds are shaken or even tipped up; sometimes fires are started. It is rare for any occupant of the house to be injured, although in a recent case reported to me by a vicar a hot water bottle flew through the air and hit the father of the house.

One example that must interest Christians is the poltergeist in the Wesley household when John Wesley's father was rector of Epworth. Southey reproduces the descriptive accounts and letters relating to this in an appendix to his *Life of Wesley*. The household was disturbed night and day by noises, the tramping of feet, and the shaking of crockery and beds, although nothing was actually moved out of place. During family prayers the noises were particularly obstreperous in the prayers for the royal family. The children referred to the entity as Old Jeffery.

It was noticed that little Hetty Wesley was twitching in her sleep, sometimes shortly before the onset of the noises. This ties up with other poltergeist manifestations where there is someone who seems to be at the centre of the manifestations. This may be a child, an emotional teenager during puberty, or an older person who is passing through a time of mental stress. In fact, one can make a case for poltergeist phenomena being a breakdown outside the body. If so, we are back at our theory of psychic force. It may be so, yet almost certainly this bursting energy is in this case being taken up and directed by a spirit entity.

The proof of this is that a poltergeist is usually exorcised by prayer and command in the name of Christ. Both the invisible spirit and the rooms in the house are 'cleansed' in this way, although naturally the person through whom the force is being drawn may need counselling and help to solve the repressed problems which are creating the energy.

A vicar recently sent me a report of a difficult case in which he, as well as the family, had experienced frightening noises and the movement of objects and furniture. He also sent me a tape recording of an interview with the family afterwards. Since the report was confidential I cannot give any details that might identify the parish or family. At first, prayer and attempts at cleansing had no effect and the phenomena grew more intense. They ceased for a time after further prayer, and then returned.

There was a most unusual ending to the story in that the spirit apologized to the family and asked for prayer. They asked whether it wanted to go to Jesus, and it replied that it did, and after the family had prayed intensely for some minutes they were conscious of a lifting of the atmosphere, and the spirit left them. The change was also felt by the dog, which previously had been uneasy and restless and had refused to go upstairs. Similarly, the Wesleys' dog appeared to sense the presence of Old Jeffery.

In this case, there were three significant facts. A young man in the house appeared to be the centre from which some force was drawn. Also the daughter had been badly upset by dabbling in spiritualism two years ago. And there had been a suicide some time previously in the house next door which was at this time being demolished. Incidentally, the spirit named itself to the girl before departing, giving the same name that a spirit had given when she was practising spiritualism. She did not divulge what the name was.

A Christian lady has sent me a newspaper report of a poltergeist case that happened in a vicarage near Malvern in 1952. She vouches for the truth of it, since she and several other Christians went to assist the vicar and curate in prayer, but once again it was a battle of weeks before the disturbances ceased. In this case the vicar was repeatedly thrown out of bed; he and his sceptical churchwarden saw a heavy chest moved; bells rang and there were weird howling noises.

A curate sent me a report of a case which was passed to the Society for Psychical Research. He was called in when a family found things being moved and rearranged in an attic room. The husband saw a broom, which he had carried upstairs, lift itself up and travel across the room. In this case their young daughter was a nervous and sensitive type of girl, and the wife suffered from depression.

On a later occasion the curate and a doctor who were spending a night in the same house saw the young daughter walking in her sleep and moving objects about, so undoubtedly she could have been physically responsible for some of the phenomena. At other times the wife was with her husband when things were moved, but her disturbed state may have produced the psychic force on these occasions. It may also be relevant that the husband's aunt had died a fortnight before the troubles first began.

I have had several long talks with Dom Robert Petitpierre, the Anglican monk with a vast amount of experience in practical encounters with the powers of evil. [He died 20 December 1982.] In his book, *Exorcising Devils* (Hale, 1976) he writes about the exorcism of places, and includes the following phenomena as predisposing causes that can be linked to evil spirits:

1. Poltergeist activity due to psychic action from some uncontrolled human subconsciousness, or to the influence of magicians, or perhaps to some non-human, mischievous sprite.

2. Haunts deliberately created by black magicians.

3. Demonic interference, often arising from habitual seances, but sometimes occurring on Christian sites that have been desecrated, or on ancient sites of pagan magic.[*]

4. Human sin, e.g. a place of bad sexual behaviour, occasionally an old fertility cult, or a place of business devoted to greed or domination, since human sin opens the door for other evil forces to enter.

---

[*] Authors original note: There is some evidence that lines of force still exist, linking pagan magic centres together across the country, and magicians are now endeavouring to use them. Another clergyman, who has had some most unpleasant experiences in dealing with haunts, confirmed this from his own experience.

28: Close the Door

I have so far confined myself mostly to examples of the occult from Britain, but a recent conversation with a Christian leader from Kenya is worth including here. His father was the first convert from his village and returned there as preacher and teacher. Gradually a church was gathered in the face of much opposition. There was a well on the edge of the forest, and this and the surrounding forest were haunted by spirits who spoke to many of the people when they went to draw water.

After the church was built, the spirits retreated and told the people before they left that it was the ringing of the church bell morning and evening that was driving them away. No doubt spirits could stand a bit of noise, but it was the Christian significance of the bell that drove them out as it called Christians to pray. The fact remains that neither Christians nor pagans heard the spirit voices any longer.

In addition to possession of places, we must consider possession of individuals by evil spirits. Again, Christian ministers who are used to exorcism recognize these, but modern thought is suspicious of the concept of demon possession. A standard work in support of the belief is the rare work by Dr JL Nevius, *Demon Possession and Allied Themes* (Revell NY, 1892), written from experiences in China.

The tendency today is to regard all the phenomena as psychological in origin. Yet Jesus Christ believed in it and distinguished between normal illnesses, to be cured by laying-on of hands or anointing, and demon-possession, to be cured by the word of command (e.g. Matthew 10:8; Mark 6:13; Luke 13:32).

Any practising psychologist who could cure 'an extensive complex of compulsive phenomena' – as such possession has been called – by a word of command would soon be a rich man, and would clear up the waiting lists that are the nightmare of psychiatry.

Even if full possession is rare in this country, obsessive attacks by spirits are likely to be met with, particularly among those who have been mixed up with the occult. In preparing this book I have been sent tragic reports of students and others who have suffered in this way. One clergyman writes of four students who after one or two seances 'were depressed, suicidal, and subject to compulsive behaviour', which included being forced to stop and stand outside certain houses. Two other girls were urged to commit suicide by spirits alleged to be their fathers, and one attempted it.

In *Viewpoint 16* (Autumn 1970) there is a vivid account of a boy in a house party who went rigid at the suggestion of a seance, and was restored only by commanding prayer. He had been inwardly attacked at an earlier seance.

How do these spirits get a footing in a human being? They obviously come in via the unconscious, and probably through the function that we call the spirit. This seems to be the way of exit and entrance for the spirit world. It is intended to be the life link with the Holy Spirit of God, but if it is unoccupied by him it can be the entrance for an evil spirit. Since man is a unity, entry here can influence any part or all parts of the personality. Normally a human being is a defended castle, but any trafficking with the spirit world lets down the drawbridge. Once the bridge is down, it is extremely difficult to close it again by an act of will. [*]

Jesus Christ, who of course understood these things, told of the danger for anyone who has had an evil spirit driven out of him. If he merely tries to keep the house of his life clean but empty, the spirit may return with others beside (Luke 11:24-26). In the previous verses Christ has led up to this diagnosis by presenting himself as the one stronger than Satan who comes to occupy the place that Satan had possessed.

I think also that deliberate sins can open the door to spirit influence, in the sense that a spirit may fasten on your habits and drive you into some evil behaviour, and perhaps force you into a breakdown. Here the disentangling from sin through Jesus Christ may itself break the spirit's grip, and even psychiatric treatment by breaking the habit could weaken the spirit's influence, though without dealing with the root cause.

---

[*] The current analogy could be the computer firewall, which must be active to prevent unauthorized access to the computer from the internet. To continue the analogy, there is also the risk to a computer user of unknowingly downloading a malicious virus or suspicious program, without adequate protection in place – in the Christian life this protection would be the indwelling Holy Spirit. But to turn off the protection and download a suspicious program willingly can lead to disaster that requires specialist help to repair.

Several times we have adopted hypotheses to guide our thinking in the light of Scripture and experience. My own theory of spirit-control is to the best of my knowledge not taken from anyone else, but it is worth considering. One of the strange things that we have already looked at is hypnotism. No one knows how it works, but the hypnotic suggestion clearly touches a control centre which then puts it into action. The suggestion may be to do something, say something or be something.

If a spirit can reach this centre, he can plant the suggestion that will then be worked out. Obviously spirits cannot do this just as they please, they must first be let in by invitation, as with the Ouija board, or by some persistent sin. The occult with its direct appeal seems to be the most usual occasion of entry. From the hypnotic centre the spirit can induce visions, voices and compulsions. Since these so frequently follow dabbling in the occult, it is obvious that the spirits that one seems to contact – father, mother, husband, wife – are not what they seem to be, since they would not cause these after-effects.

Most of these spirits are content with obsession (a kind of haunting), getting malicious satisfaction out of upsetting their victim. Occasionally they can implant a major controlling idea that changes the whole personality, and since they are now riding the victim they produce what is called demon-possession. In this, they get the satisfaction of using the body by a semi-incarnation.

If we ask why they do not always go to the limit, the Scriptural answer is probably found in Job 1:12 and Luke 22:31-32, where Satan is allowed to affect human lives, but has a limit imposed by God beyond which he cannot go. So the mercy of God curbs the power of individual attacks on the control centre, even though he has made man so that any emptiness of spirit is a tacit invitation to attack and invasion (compare Matthew 12:43-45), and any direct approach to the spirit world is the exercise of man's free choice to invite the spirits to come in. The vital thing is that obsession and possession are facts, whether or not the analogy with hypnotism is worth following up.

Vic Ramsey of New Life Foundation writes in *Viewpoint 16*, 'From our own experience over the past six years we have witnessed a serious interest in the occult among drug takers.'

It is likely that these drugs can act as an opener up for evil spirits to come in at a deep level, since drugs, apart from being evil in themselves, lower the God-given barriers that consciousness sets up. Certainly the initiation of many shamans and witch doctors, leading to deliberate possession, is assisted by drugs.

I personally wonder how much addictive craving is then produced by evil spirits, so that they can share physical and emotional experiences that are otherwise denied to them. One might compare the way sexually inhibited humans look for vicarious yet shared satisfaction through pornographic pictures and books.

Someone who is competent to do it might well investigate the effect of some rhythms and music for good or bad. Like every gift of God, music has its uplift and its degradation. Just as drugs can induce possession, so certain rhythms and drummings can do the same. Voodoo is an excellent example, and there is no better book on the subject than Maya Deren's *Divine Horsemen* (Thames and Hudson, 1953). Maya Deren went as a student of Haitian religion, and ended by getting 'hooked' herself.

157

One is often asked whether a Christian can become possessed. Any Christian who at any time opens up the door to spirits is in danger of being disturbed by them afterwards. He has done something that cannot simply be shrugged off and forgotten. However, experience suggests that this disturbance is more likely to follow several contacts than a single attempt which may be made quite innocently. No one who has read this book could now dabble innocently.

Christians in this country, who before conversion have been involved in magic, have had spiritual, psychic and physical battering after conversion. They have been threatened by spells from former colleagues, and have had to call on other Christians to fight in prayer to keep the door closed to spirit interference.

Missionaries who are familiar with possession tell how converts have burned their idols and charms after having had evil spirits cast out of their bodies. Destruction by burning is important, since the idols definitely absorb evil. But if the converts have later returned to idol worship, they have again become possessed.

The Bible shows that God brings or allows some punishments in order to recall his people to their senses. This for example is the biblical interpretation of the exile in Babylon. So although we cannot escape the defiance of spiritual laws any more than physical, God can temper them for our good.

If I lay myself open to spirit invasion I shall very likely have disturbing and frightening experiences; but if I have previously known the power of God in my life, I may see what I am doing and quickly turn back to him in confession, and ask him to throw back the spirits and close the gate. If I persist with the spirits, I shall be in much more serious danger.

In some quarters there is a tendency to treat any beset-ting sin as a case for exorcism. The danger is that if the person is relieved, he may have the half unconscious feeling that the demon, and not himself, was the guilty party.

One of the most balanced and informative books on deliverance is *But deliver us from Evil* (Darton, 1974). The author, John Richards, was given a year's leave for special study of the subject, and had personal links with all sorts of Christians who have had some experience in delivering others.

I have several times mentioned Dom Robert Petitpi-erre, the Anglican Benedictine monk, and his book *Exorcising Devils* (Hale, 1976) is a lively personal account of what has been his special calling.

Specifically evangelical books include, John Richards' *Exorcism, Deliverance and Healing: some pastoral guidelines* (Grove Books, 1976) and Don Basham's *Deliver us from Evil* (Hodder and Stoughton, 1973).

It is only fair to mention William Sargant's book, *The Mind Possessed* (Lippincott, 1974) which explains possession in terms of body responses to stress and suggestion. The book is useful for the personal experiences of Dr Sargant in many parts of the world, but I believe that we are often faced with a *both/and* rather than an *either/or*. Spirits can enter when invited, and use the body mechanisms.

29: What Should I Do?

Many readers will not be personally involved in the occult, and will be happy to stay that way. But for others the subject is far more immediately relevant, since they or their friends have been or could be involved in some way. What should they do about it?

I say 'could be', so that we can start now to beware of even beginning. Do not attempt to make any contact with any spirits, whether through mediums, Ouija boards, sliding tumblers, automatic writing or magic. If you do, you are deliberately trying something upon which God has put an invariable ban in Scripture. And to repeat an earlier warning, do not be caught by the argument that other things are forbidden in the Old Testament that Christians allow today, such as eating bacon.

As we have seen, if communications with the departed were of benefit to them or to us, they would be so important that the New Testament at least would have lifted the Old Testament ban and encouraged us to help one another in this way. But although it modifies some of the social regulations of the Old Testament, the New Testament *never* withdraws the ban on contacting spirits.

We are not being narrow and obstructive. In these days there is hardly one biblical command that is not challenged. God's word about fornication and adultery is being disputed, even by writers who profess the Christian standpoint. Many of our accepted standards have dropped to the levels of Greece and Rome. The punishment that must follow as an inevitable result is the decay of both individual and society. It is God's punishment, but it is not arbitrary.

In this book we have distinguished between deliberately contacting the spirits from our side, and accepting occasional unsought and generally unrepeated appearances of a loved one around the time of their death. When Jesus Christ appeared to his disciples after his resurrection, they thought he was a ghost. Jesus did not reply that there were no such things as ghosts, but said that 'no ghost has flesh and bones as you can see that I have' (Luke 24:39 NEB).

If your 'drowned friend' appears to you, he is out of the body. When Jesus appeared, he was *in* the body, although when his body rose from the grave it was transformed so as — to have new properties that it did not have before.

What are we to say about second sight in general? We are on more difficult ground here, and Christians are divided over our attitude to it. Since I have been writing this book I have found several Christians who have this gift occasionally, and who have been relieved to find me talking about it naturally. On the other hand, an experienced Christian minister who made valuable suggestions when he read this book in manuscript, is emphatic that a Christian should pray for the faculty to be removed. A Christian whose mother had second sight told me that she found it worrying. Obviously, the proper thing is to pray that if the 'gift' is not according to the will of God, he will take it away. If then it persists, we take it that he will use it if it is put into his hands.

A danger is that a spiritualist will sense that you have this gift and will urge you to develop it in spiritualist circles. Obviously this is wrong. Or you could be tempted to develop it yourself by crystal gazing, or take up some form of fortune-telling. Why would this be wrong? Because you do not become more useful to God, to yourself, or to your fellow humans by trying to foretell the future – which is what developing second sight leads to, even when it does not deliberately invoke spirits.

Second sight may be thought of as presenting dangers similar to those of the gift of sex, in the modern rather restricted sense of the word. The joy of sex is a vital part of marriage, but when sex is developed as a thing in itself it becomes degrading and shabby. Similarly, second sight even in its mildest forms is an ingredient of life that God can use only as we go straight ahead with him. Its cultivation for its own sake leads to bypaths, and may spoil our inner and outer life.

Although the average person wants to use those who have second sight for foretelling the future, we feel wary of doing so for ourselves or others. These desires should be turned into prayer, just as we pray when a friend tells us of some need in a letter. If we have a tendency to pick up atmospheres as a general sensation or in picture form, we shall be more sensitive to hauntings, but we will also be quicker to detect the inner needs of people whom we meet. I will not go further into this, but some readers will know the sort of things that I mean. I repeat again that I do not have these experiences myself.

Since I have suggested that some of the communications from mediums and the Ouija board are telepathic and clairvoyant in origin, it may be argued that these do not come under the biblical ban. Let us be clear about one basic fact: those who use these means, are testing to see whether they can contact spirits. They are not wanting to draw on the unconscious minds of themselves and the other participants. Suppose that what emerges is the product of their own minds, they are still being deceived by the apparent source of the messages in the spirit world.

Experience shows that what emerges soon becomes a conglomeration of evil, even if it starts apparently harmlessly. I do not want to break down God-given barriers and allow a group evil to flow in and out, as it must do if a telepathic linkage is opened up.

This emergence of evil was brought home to me recently at a university conference when I was asked to speak on 'The Realm of the Psychic'. In conversations afterwards, with agnostics as well as Christians, everyone who spoke to me told of the degrading effect that these practices had had on their acquaintances. No one defended them. It would seem that the entity which communicates could be understood as a personalization of everybody's evil which can then flow back into individuals, leaving them worse than before. But one must return to the *both/and* rather than the *either/or*. If evil spirits exist, they will make use of the dropping of the barriers, and take up and use the latent psychic capacities in those who have invited them in.

What if we have already been involved ourselves, or want to help those who have been involved and who come to ask us for help? For ourselves, we must ask for prayer from our Christian friends, and claim the victory of Christ for the whole of our being.

Apart from what we have done ourselves, we may from time to time have to face some unpleasant manifestation of the occult. On several occasions members of Christian Unions have encountered the results of seances in their colleges or halls of residence. These results may take the form of a well-defined sense of evil in some of the rooms and passages.

Since non-Christian students have been responsible for letting these powers loose, it has seemed reasonable to suggest that Christian students should prove the power of Christ as stronger. Members of the Christian Union have mobilized effective prayer, and Christ through them has removed the hauntings. Naturally, if the seances continue, the trouble will come again, but sometimes discerning Christian have broken up the communications by holding a prayer meeting at the time when a seance is being held.

Ministers are asked to help in unusual cases, and can usually put people in touch with someone who is experienced in dealing with occult manifestations, and whose gift is that of 1 Corinthians 12:10: 'the ability to distinguish between spirits', coupled with the capacity to deal with them by exorcism or other means.

Yet one must remember that it is not the superior magic of the exorcist, but the power of Christ that overcomes the spirit. Ministers have told me of how God has used them in exorcism without any special gifts; they have simply acted according to Scripture.

Some exorcists use adaptations of traditional Roman Catholic methods, including the sprinkling of holy water and salt that has been blessed, and some even use old Latin prayers, though one cannot see why a spirit should know Latin rather than English if it has chosen to manifest itself in England. I personally am not convinced that these things are the effective agents, and certainly they could not be a substitute for the name of Jesus Christ, which of course these exorcists use.

30: Being Prepared

A few weeks ago a clergyman wrote to me about a case which shows how someone without previous experience was able to act simply and effectively. In visiting a country cottage, Mrs X several times 'saw' a lady in Tudor costume, generally accompanied by a large dog with a harness collar. The lady 'told' Mrs X that her baby, conceived by someone other than her husband, had been murdered and thrown into a well. She was distressed that it had not been baptized, and asked Mrs X to find a priest to sprinkle holy water over the spot where the well used to be.

Soon the lady began to appear to Mrs X in her own home, although her dog did not come when Mrs X's dog was in the room! Finally, Mr and Mrs X felt that the matter must be resolved and got in touch with their vicar whom I know well. He went to their home, and speaking about the power of the Lord Jesus Christ told them that he did not think that holy water was the answer, but that 'only the living Christ who spanned all time could release anyone from this kind of trouble, and that we could be assured that the soul of the murdered baby has been accepted by Jesus, and covered by his work once for all on the cross.'

While he was talking, he took out his New Testament. At this point Mrs X 'fainted', or presumably went into a light trance. She repeated that the lady was present, and passed on to her what the vicar had said. As she came round, her tense expression had changed to one of peace, and she told her husband, 'Isn't it wonderful! She is happy now, and everything is all right'. I have since heard again that all is well.

Here is something that was dealt with quite simply in the name of Jesus Christ, without anyone having to understand the way it all worked. Indeed, one might discuss the case at considerable length and still not understand it, especially if we include the dog and its harness!

More skilled advice may be needed if black magic is involved. I do not myself understand the technicalities of black magic, but know there is far more to it than most people realize. Even so, Christ's victory is the defence, though the knowledge of all that is involved in the threat, haunting or activity, is undoubtedly of extra assistance.

Some further discernment is also useful with poltergeists. We have already discussed in chapter 27 the problem of understanding whether it is a person or a place that needs to be cleaned up. Does the person affect the place, or the place the person, in any one instance? If the person is the centre, is psychological help needed as well as the vital cleansing of spirit or from spirit? Nevertheless, I know that 'unskilled' ministers have cleansed such poltergeistic activities in the name of Jesus Christ.

Any Christian who is called in to help, must themselves be in right relationship with God. They are to take part in a spiritual operation, and must not be like a surgeon with an open wound on his hands trying to operate on a deep infection without gloves. Or to change the picture, a Christian cannot go into battle against an evil spirit with a large area of his life in alliance with the enemy. They first must confess their known and unknown sins, and claim the cleansing of the blood of Jesus Christ.

If possible, a Christian should have others joining in prayer either in the same room or at the same time. Prayer should be for the person, or for the driving out of the spirit or the evil from the place. The point about 'the evil' is that this may be an imprinted atmosphere from past or present.

At some point the spirit must be told in the name of the Lord Jesus, who won the victory on the cross and rose again victoriously as the Head of every principality and power, to depart, to go to its own place, and there abide for ever. A cordon of prayer should be thrown round all present, to prevent the spirit transferring to a new host. Almost certainly this was the reason for Christ's sending of the demons into the Gadarene swine; the danger of releasing a legion of them into the crowd was very real.

To some hard-boiled readers all this will seem like fantasy, yet one day they may meet some of the phenomena we have been thinking about. When one has dismissed the fraud, the faulty observation, credulity and suggestion that make natural happenings look like supernatural, there is enough evidence left to show that really nasty things are happening today, as they have done down the ages. Science as such cannot touch them. Magic may be met by counter-magic, but only Christ can cure by conquest.

We must always return to the reality of the Lord Jesus Christ. He was not a reincarnated man, nor a spirit being, nor a good man filled with the Spirit of God. He is true God who became Man by genuine though unique conception and birth. His purpose in coming was to undo the effects of sin, to put away our guilt by bearing our sins in his sacrificial death on the cross, and to make us clean before renewing us by the inpoured life of his Spirit.

Christians would never presume to claim what they do claim, if it were not that God has promised it. The Person and work of Jesus Christ are far wider and more glorious than any spiritualist or occultist ever imagines.

31: Out-of-Body Experiences

We turn next to unusual body experiences. A number of people have had an OBE – not the medal, but shorthand for Out-of-Body Experience. At a time of unconsciousness, or even after apparent death, people have found themselves looking down on their own body, or even travelling away from it. After regaining consciousness they have described what they saw being done to their body. Sometimes they have spoken of a journey through a tunnel into light, right up to a form of barrier. They often claim that they knew that if they crossed this barrier they could not return to the body again.

Several writers have investigated these cases. It makes sense to suppose that if the centre of personality can be detached from the body now, it also continues to exist after the death of the body. As we have seen earlier, this does not of course prove the Christian belief in survival; it only gives evidence of temporary survival.

There is nothing strictly equivalent to an OBE in the Bible, though there is something approaching it in the experience of the prophet Ezekiel. He was among the Israelites exiled in Babylon before Jerusalem had been destroyed by the Babylonians. He tells how the Spirit of God 'lifted me up between earth and heaven, and in visions of God he took me to Jerusalem' (Ezekiel 40:2 NIV).

Ezekiel describes the sensation of a hand picking him up by a lock of his hair. When he found himself in Jerusalem he was told where to go and what to see, and he even seemed to dig a hole and pass through a door into a secret room where pagan ceremonies were being conducted. At one point he was given a peep behind the scenes as God marked out those who would be saved and those who would be lost in the coming destruction (Ezekiel chapters 8 and 9).

These experiences can fairly be described as OBEs, since it is implied that Ezekiel's body remained in Babylon, and that he was invisible to the people in Jerusalem. The unseen personality that leaves the body in an ordinary OBE is presumably the same as the personality which left Ezekiel's body.

However, we must admit that the experience was different from that which people have experienced after an accident or in the operating theatre. Ezekiel had not been involved in an accident, but was sitting with friends to whom he appeared to be in a trance, a state they would take for granted since he was a prophet.

If we must give Ezekiel's OBE a label, it was probably an example of travelling clairvoyance, an experience in which a person travels in perception to a distance place, while the body remains consciously in the same place.

There is a striking example of travelling clairvoyance in the autobiography of Mrs Eileen Garrett [1893-1970]. Mrs

Garrett was much more than a medium, and it was she who ultimately came to doubt the genuineness of the spirits which claimed to communicate through her. She was a remarkable psychic who allowed herself to be tested in all kinds of ways. In one test conducted in New York [in 1932], she set out to 'travel' to a doctor in Newfoundland who knew the experiment was in progress. A group of friends in New York noted everything she said.

Mrs Garrett came to the doctor's house, described his garden and flowers, passed through the walls of the house into the selected room, and saw the doctor enter with a bandage wrapped round his head. No one in New York knew he had been in an accident, and they were surprised when she reported the bandage to them.

Mrs Garrett went on to describe objects that the doctor had set out on his table, and telepathised what he was reading silently to himself. After the experiment, people at both ends wrote a full description of the events as they had experienced them. The letters crossed in the post – and tallied.

Ezekiel apparently had a similar, though not identical, experience. God drew him out of his body because he wished the exiles to know the decadent state of many of those left in Jerusalem. This might lessen the shock when the city was destroyed.

There are well-authenticated instances of Christians levitating. For example, Joseph of Copertino [1603-1663] used to float in the air in a state of ecstasy – both in a chapel and outside. The sight turned Friedrich Duke of Brunswick from a Lutheran to a Catholic. Reliable observers saw DD Home, whom we have mentioned as handling fire, levitating on more than one occasion.

Coming now to the mystery of body transportation, the prophet Elijah was parted from Elisha by a chariot of fire and went up by a whirlwind into heaven (2 Kings 2). Unless we regard the chariot as a UFO, it is difficult to explain what happened to Elijah. Although I take it he was mysteriously levitated, the biblical description need mean no more than that the whirlwind took him away bodily after the chariot had separated Elisha from the whirlwind. At some point in the upper atmosphere ('heaven' here is clearly the sky) Elijah must have died, but his grave is as unknown as that of Moses whom God buried (Deuteronomy 34:6).

The other example of teleportation comes in the New Testament. In Acts 8:26-40 the apostle Philip meets an Ethiopian in the desert and explains to him the gospel of Jesus Christ. Eventually he baptizes the Ethiopian, after which 'the Spirit of the Lord suddenly took Philip away; and the eunuch did not see him again ... Philip, however, appeared at Azotus' (Acts 8:39-40 NIV).

There is little doubt that this means Philip was miraculously transported to Azotus. One commentator prefers, 'the Spirit of the Lord suddenly took Philip from the scene', implying that he was simply guided away. But the normal use of the Greek verb justifies the translation 'caught up' or 'took', and it is used in this way of the apostle Paul being caught up to heaven in a vision (2 Corinthians 12:2).

Probably most of us are sceptical of claims to teleportation [bi-location] of this kind, but there is some evidence for it outside the Bible. Spanish records tell of a soldier who on 25 October 1593 suddenly appeared in Mexico City in the uniform of a regiment stationed in Manila [approximately 9,000 miles, over 14,000 km, away]. At his trial for magic practices before the Inquisition he swore that the last thing he knew was being on sentry duty outside the Governor's palace [in the Philippines]. He claimed that the governor had just been assassinated, a fact that was as yet unknown in Mexico City.[*]

A still more puzzling story concerns Sister Mary of Ágreda in Spain, [born on April 2, 1602]. She never left her Spanish convent, yet between 1620 and 1631 she 'travelled' to New Mexico, [also reportedly to what is known today as Texas and Arizona], and converted many Jumano Indians to Christ. The Catholic authorities attempted to suppress her claims, until the head of the mission in New Mexico [Father Benavides] wrote to the pope asking who had preceded him in his mission.

The Native Indians apparently claimed that they had been converted through a lady dressed in blue [who gave out Christian religious items, which the head of the mission reportedly identified]. When the head of the mission returned to Spain he met Sister Mary; her description of the Indians and their customs tallied with his own knowledge of them. Her 'travels' were attested by Spanish conquistadors, French explorers and various Indian tribes.

We cannot close this chapter without considering the resurrection of Jesus Christ. This certainly was the coming to life again of Jesus with his body, although that body had new capacities such as being able to appear and disappear, and to pass through closed doors. Jesus himself made it clear that he was not a ghost; he told his disciples 'a ghost

---

[*] The soldier's name is recorded as Gil Pérez. It was reported that it was two months before news of the governor's death reached Mexico. When it did, not only was the event confirmed, but also many details of Gil Pérez's story. The ship carrying the news also brought at least one witness who confirmed seeing Gil Pérez in Manila on October 23.

does not have flesh and bones, as you see I have.' He then demonstrated the difference, by eating food in front of them (Luke 24:37-43 NIV).

Some people believe Jesus survived in spirit only, and point out the difficulty of reconciling the different Gospel accounts of the discovery of the empty tomb. But there is more than one way of bringing these stories together satisfactorily, and there is no doubt that the tomb was empty. Although some critics claim that the apostle Paul does not rest his argument upon the empty tomb. In fact, he does so every time he uses the term 'resurrection' and 'risen', for no Jew or Greek could use these words if the body was still in the tomb.

If the Jews had removed the body, they could have demolished the preaching of the disciples by producing it. If the disciples had stolen it, they would scarcely have suffered as they did for the sake of a lie. If Jesus had revived in the tomb and rolled aside the great stone, he would have needed months to recover and could never have appeared as the triumphant victor over death.

It is impossible to find a parallel, as we have tried to do in other instances. There are a number of resurrection stories in the Bible, but in all of the others the body was brought to life again and was only restored as before, and eventually the person died again. But Jesus Christ rose to die no more.

Passing from the historical mystery of the resurrection of Jesus Christ, we have the future mystery of the resurrection of all Christians, that we have already looked at briefly in an earlier chapter. Although those who have passed on are 'with Christ', they are still incomplete human beings. We cannot tell how they experience the passage of time, but we know that the Second Coming of Christ in time is still to come. It is at that Second Coming that 'the dead in Christ will rise' (1 Thessalonians 4:16), and 'the Lord Jesus Christ will transform our lowly bodies so that they will be like his glorious body' (Philippians 3:21).

So whatever form the miracle may take, it is part and parcel of our being in Christ. His body has already been raised and transformed. Those of us who are alive at the Second Coming will be instantly transformed, without having to pass through the intermediate state of nakedness without a body.

This is the picture that Paul uses in 2 Corinthians 5:1-10. Although death apart from the body is to be 'at home with the Lord', it is nonetheless to be incomplete, and naked, until we receive our resurrection bodies at the Second Coming of Jesus Christ.

The Bible never despises the body as though it were a mere prison house. God created us not as pure spirits but as beings of spirit, mind and body, to glorify him. One day we shall be restored, so that death does not have the last word. It is hard enough to grasp the mysteries of the past, and it is impossible to grasp this mystery which is yet to come. But one day we shall know.

In this chapter I have not included the ascension of Jesus Christ as an example of teleportation or psychic levitation (Acts 1:9). It certainly was a levitation, and Luke, the careful historian, had plenty of opportunity in his travels to discover from members of the Twelve what they actually saw and heard. This was a wholly divine action, a visible conclusion to Christ's ministry on earth for the time being. Some Christians find a partial similarity in the assumption to heaven of the Virgin Mary, although this lacks the evidence of contemporary eyewitnesses such as we have for Christ's ascension.

For reference:
John Allan: *A Book of Mysteries,* (Lion Publishing, 1981)
John Michell & Robert Rickard: *Phenomena,* (Thames & Hudson, 1979)
Hans Eysenck & Carl Sargent: *Explaining the Unexplained* (Weidenfeld & Nicolson, 1982)
Maurice Rawlings: *Beyond Death's Door,* (Sheldon, 1979)
Eileen Garrett: *My Life as a Search for the Meaning of Mediumship,* (Rider, 1939). Also, *Many Voices,* (Allen & Unwin, 1969)
EJ Dingwall: *Some Human Oddities,* (Home & Van Thai, 1947)
John Wenham, *Easter Enigma,* (Paternoster Press, 1984)

32: The Stars

Astrology began with astronomy, the observation of the heavens. The word *astronomy* means the *laws* governing the stars, while *astrology* is the *meaning* of the stars in relation to mankind. The modern astrologer need never look at the skies at all; he can work entirely from charts.

Around 3000 BC the Egyptians noted the summer solstice by the rising at dawn of the star Sirius, then known as *Sothis*. Later, the Babylonians recorded the rising and setting of the planet Venus. In the Old Testament the New Moon marks the beginning of the month, and the Passover in both the Old and New Testaments is celebrated at the spring Full Moon.

This is all astronomy, and it is this that Genesis chapter 1 refers to: 'And God said, "Let there be lights in the expanse of the sky to separate the day from the night, and let them serve as signs to mark seasons and days and years..."' (1:14 NIV).

Astrology began when people started to look for meanings in some of the movements of the planets against the fixed pattern of the stars. In the middle of the seventh century BC the approach of Venus to the constellation Virgo was regarded as a sign of approaching disaster. When Mars approached Jupiter it was believed there would be devastation in the land. The movements of the moon among the constellations and planets were easily observed and given special meaning. Presumably actual events were noted, and it was assumed that what had occurred once would occur again when the heavenly bodies were in a similar position.

In these early times the signs were applied to national events rather than to individuals – except for kings, as representing their people. This is how the prophet Isaiah viewed astrology when he foretold the doom of Babylon. 'Let your astrologers come forward, those stargazers who make predictions month by month, let them save you from what is coming upon you' (Isaiah 47:13 NIV). Isaiah and Jeremiah always look behind the stars to the Creator of the stars.

It is uncertain when individual horoscopes based on birthdates began. Probably it originated as advice about good or bad days for an individual to take some important step. In Imperial Rome deductions were drawn from the sign of the Zodiac under which a person was born, and the emperors Augustus, Tiberius, Caligula and Claudius all had court astrologers to advise them concerning the position of the planets in relation to their sun sign. Probably their advice was much the same as is found in our newspapers, since this is also based on the sun signs.

Astrologers gradually moved towards more detailed horoscopes, until today it is regarded as essential to know the exact moment of birth, and also the longitude of the birthplace for an accurate horoscope to be drawn up.

Astrologers are divided in their emphases on whether the planets, sun and moon actually affect a person's life, or whether their positions merely indicate the internal and external influences that a person is encountering from birth and at a particular moment. The former view began with the linking of the planets with powerful gods and goddesses. This underlies the warning in Deuteronomy 4:19 not to worship the host of heaven and treat them as gods.

In spite of this warning, some of the prophet Jeremiah's opponents were people who made 'cakes for the queen of heaven' (Jeremiah 7:18), and who after the destruction of Jerusalem blamed the temporary abandonment of their worship of the queen of heaven for the disasters that had come (Jeremiah 44:15-25).

The 'queen of heaven' was Ishtar, or Venus. Similarly, the northern kingdom of Israel is denounced for worshipping a star-god Kaiwan, probably Saturn. Amos declares that instead of the images of Saturn and another god being able to help, their worshippers would carry them into exile (Amos 5:26-27).

Later, Jewish writers made a kind of compromise by allotting an angel to each star. They justified this by the use of the title 'the hosts of heaven' for the stars (Deuteronomy 4:19, Isaiah 34:4 RSV) and also for the angels (1 Kings 22:19 RSV). In addition, the angels are described as 'the morning stars' (Job 38:7).

Daniel was appointed head of the college of wise men including astrologers in Babylon (Daniel 2:48). This does not mean he himself practised astrology; in fact the book of Daniel demonstrates the inability of the astrologers to interpret Nebuchadnezzar's dream (Daniel 2:1-11), whereas

God revealed the interpretation to Daniel.

Is there anything in this belief that has been held for so long? It is difficult for Christians to believe that their lives are governed by the position of the planets. This would be to fly in the face of all that the prophets say about God as creator and upholder of the heavenly bodies. However, it is possible that the time of the year when we are born may indicate certain trends of character.

If this is true, I would take it to be an extension of the 'calendar' purpose of the heavenly bodies. But it may be no more than coincidence, and the only way to show that it is anything more would be to give the description of each sign to various people and ask them to match them against their friends whose birth dates they do not know.

If the correct results were no more than we would expect by chance, astrologers would claim that the position and aspects of the planets at the moment of birth have to be taken into account, as well as the position of the sun.

We may perhaps link this to Jung's concept of synchronicity, that is meaningful coincidence. Most writers nowadays refer to the work of Michel Gauquelin [1928-1991], who discovered that there is a strong tendency for medical men to have been born when either Mars or Saturn was rising. He found correlations with some other professions, too. But unlike astrologers, he maintains that what counts is the actual time of birth, irrespective of the date or place. What matters is the planet that was rising at the moment.

Personally, I would not go to an astrologer to have a reading of my progressed horoscope which claims to show how I am being influenced now and in the future. The interpretation may be right, and I have no doubt that interpretations may be given by clairvoyance, the horoscope providing a link with the person himself. But I must stress that I do not believe God means us to guide our lives by the predictions of astrology, cards or crystal balls.

There is another great Bible mystery, centring on the identity of the Magi and the nature of the star in the east recorded in Matthew chapter 2. Contrary to popular belief, the Bible does not say that the Magi were kings, nor that there were three of them. But tradition may be correct, and in any case it would be churlish to spoil good Christmas carols and hymns with arguments based on no further evidence.

Nowadays we often use the Greek word *Magi* to describe the visitors, even though elsewhere in Greek literature of this date the word means *magician*. The RSV retains the traditional translation *wise men*, which is justified if we understand that their wisdom included a search for the meaning of life by observation of the universe. The NEB is misleading when it describes them as astrologers, since their observation of the star in this case differed from the methods used by astrologers.

We must not be misled by the later use of the word *magi*. The original Magians of the seventh century BC were a tribe in Media who formed a priesthood. They finally merged with the Zoroastrian religion which had much in common with Judaism. A Magian was an officer under King Nebuchadnezzar.

The prophet Jeremiah, in naming the Babylonian officers who captured Jerusalem, describes one of them as the *Rabmag*, or Head of the Magi (Jeremiah 39:3-13 RSV). It is probably best to retain the word Magi in Matthew 2 – alternatives include wise men, Magian priests or simply

Medians.

The Magi were obviously keen observers of possible signs in the heavens, and it is quite likely that since the time of Daniel, who was appointed as head of the College of Wise Men, they had become familiar with the Jewish belief in the coming Messiah. In particular, they may have known the prophecy that 'a star will come out of Jacob' (Numbers 24:17). So when they observed a strange phenomenon among the stars they concluded that the King of the Jews had at last been born. This was presumably not a purely intellectual deduction, but the prompting came from God, just as later they were warned in a dream not to go back to King Herod.

There has naturally been much discussion about the star itself. Most people today believe that Jesus was born between 6 and 4 BC, since King Herod, who was reigning when Jesus was born, died in 4 BC. The date of 1 AD, fixed by a sixth century writer, is clearly erroneous.

Various suggestions have been made about the star. One possible explanation is that it was a comet. Halley's comet appeared in 11 BC, but that would be too early, so we would need to postulate an otherwise unknown comet.

Another suggestion is that it was a nova, caused when the sudden explosion of a star makes it blaze brightly for a short time. This explanation was suggested by three astronomers in 1977. They believed that if the star of the Magi existed, there would be other records of a new star elsewhere. They found what they were looking for in Chinese records of 5 BC.

Another astronomer, David Hughes in *The Star of Bethlehem* (Walker and Co, NY, 1979), revived a theory that had first been suggested by Kepler in 1603, namely that the phenomenon resulted from the conjunction of the planets Jupiter and Saturn in the constellation of Pisces, which recurred three times in the space of just a few months. A computer calculation showed that Mars also came into the conjunction, and the conjunction of these three planets occurs only once every 805 years. Saturn and Pisces were both linked to the Jews, in which case 'his star' would have been Saturn, one of the three.

A minority view is that the star was some miraculous appearance; since how could a nova or Saturn 'stop over the place where the child was'? This used to puzzle me until I found the answer in Wordsworth's series of *Lucy Poems*. In the poem that begins, 'Strange fits of passion …' he describes his ride by night to Lucy's house while he watches the moon descending until it drops behind the house. I suggest that at a certain point in their ride into Bethlehem the Magi saw the star virtually touching the house where Mary, Joseph and the baby were staying.

We do not know when the star first appeared, nor how long the journey took. But since Herod ordered the massacre of all babies under two years of age, and not simply newborn babies, it is likely that the Magi arrived when Jesus was at least one year old. Mary and Joseph had evidently taken a house in Bethlehem, presumably because they did not want to call attention to the fact that Jesus had been conceived before the marriage, as would have been obvious if they had returned to Nazareth immediately.

33: Sun Mysteries

The Bible contains three mysteries concerning the sun. One is its darkening while Jesus Christ was on the cross. This could not have been an eclipse, since an eclipse of the sun can happen only at the new moon. My own belief is that it was a projection of the agony of the Sin-bearer out on to the universe. Jesus Christ is the one 'in whom all things hold together' (Colossians 1:17), and he could not take the sins of the world into himself without 'all things' being affected. Similarly, his death produced an earthquake, and also the tearing of the curtain which barred the way into the holy of holies in the temple (Matthew 27:45,51).

Peter used these events in his sermon on the day of Pentecost (Acts 2:19-20) when he quoted from the prophet Joel. Most commentators assume that the verses refer to the Second Coming, but there would be little evidential value in this. Peter is saying, 'You have seen this prophecy fulfilled. You have seen the promised pouring out of the Holy Spirit, and you have seen the physical phenomena that according to Joel herald the beginning of the day of the Lord.'

The quotation in Joel 2:30-31 speaks of the sun being turned into darkness. It also says that the moon will be turned to blood. Particles in the atmosphere can affect the colour of the moon, and the 'billows of smoke' – possibly dust caused by the earthquake – could have given a red colour to the moon at its rising. The fire mentioned would be household fires, started through the earthquake. The other sign, the blood, is clearly the blood shed by Christ on the cross.

There are two other incidents concerning the sun that read as miracles. One is often referred to as 'Joshua's long day' (Joshua 10:12-14). The Israelites were coming to the rescue of the Gibeonites from the Amorites. In the pursuit that followed, Joshua prayed, 'Sun, stand still over Gibeon, and you, moon, over the Valley of Aijalon.' This is described in the Bible as a quotation from a lost poetical work, the book of Jashar. The poem continues: 'So the sun stood still, and the moon stopped.' A prose comment adds, 'The sun stopped in the middle of the sky, and delayed going down about a full day'.

Obviously the sudden cessation of the earth's rotation, which would make the sun appear to stand still in the sky, would cause everyone to fly off the earth's surface. Therefore we must look for some interpretation of the words that presents a different picture.

The first part of the quotation is poetry, and poetry can use highly coloured descriptions which are not meant to be taken literally. For example, it might mean that daylight lasted long enough to cover the pursuit. But what about the prose? There may be a clue in the report of the 'great stones from heaven' that fell on the Amorites (Joshua 10:11 RSV). After the fall of the great meteorite in Siberia in 1908, it was noticed that the refraction from meteoric dust led to an extension of daylight in Europe.

It is certainly a strange coincidence that the record here links the extension of Joshua's day with a fall of meteorites. The dust, of course, was not thrown up from the earth, but was an accompaniment of the meteors as they travelled through space. In this way the sun's light was prolonged by refraction, even when the day should have ended.[*]

Other scholars have taken a very different view and have pictured the Israelites as scorched by the heat; Joshua commands the sun to 'be silent' – the literal meaning of 'stand still'. The sky suddenly became black with clouds, and for the rest of the day the sun did not appear out of the clouds. However, in the prose comment the word 'stopped' is not the same as the poetry 'be silent', but means 'stood'. Nevertheless, the interpretation would hold true if the sun stayed behind a cloud.

We need not worry too much about the reference to the moon in this passage. It supplies a poetic balance, and is not mentioned in the prose comment that follows. Yet it offers some evidence of an eyewitness who saw the moon over Aijalon at the time of the battle. We need to read Joshua 10:14 carefully. 'There has never been a day like it before or since, a day when the LORD listened to a man'

---

[*] The Siberian explosion at Tunguska in June 1908 is now thought to have been caused by the air burst of a large meteoroid or comet fragment at an altitude of 3-6 miles (5–10 km) above the Earth's surface, which accounts for the dust, and makes the above theory of a meteorite fall in Joshua's experience even more plausible. The Edinburgh Observatory at the time described the night as very striking, 'practically daylight, while in the north of England men are reported to have worked in the fields all night, getting in the hay' (*Popular Astronomy*, Vol. 41, November 1933, page 477).

(NIV). The point of the verse is that Joshua took it upon himself not to pray, but to command the elements, and the Lord obeyed him.

The third sun reference is in 2 Kings 20:8-11 and Isaiah 38:7-8. Here, God gives King Hezekiah a sign that he will recover from a serious illness. He makes the shadow of the sun go back ten steps or degrees on the dial measuring the time. No one knows what was the form of 'the dial of Ahaz', as it is called in Isaiah. To regard it as a series of staircase steps would be to make the divisions of time so large as to be virtually useless.

We cannot tell how much space went to form a degree, but ten degrees would certainly have been wide enough to constitute a sign. The story speaks only of the shadow, and not of the sun.

The effect could have come through something that we have all occasionally observed: when a cloud with a sharp edge covers the sun, the light that comes over the edge may be bright enough to cast a shadow, not as bright as the direct sun, but enough to register. If this is what happened on this occasion, the miracle was one of synchronisation, and the effect occurred at the moment when Isaiah and Hezekiah were looking for it.

34: The Mystery of the Coming King

To Christians down the ages, it has been no mystery that the Bible announces so much about the coming Messiah, long before he came. Handel's oratorio *Messiah* has reminded us of the prophecies which have always been accepted as inspired by God. Yet there has been a modern trend to deny the gift of prediction to the prophets, and so to give all the Messianic prophecies a reference to the prophet's own time.

But acting on the words of Jesus Christ that the prophets spoke of him (Luke 24:27,44), and on Peter's statement that the prophets were often puzzled as to the time to which their words applied (1 Peter 1:10-12), we must take a serious look at the alleged Messianic prophecies. These give three marks by which the Messiah would be recognised when he came.

1. He would be a descendant of David. David was told that his descendants would continue to rule (2 Samuel 7:12-16; Psalm 89:3-4). But bad kings and a bad people led

to the remedial punishment of the Jews by the exile.

On the eve of the exile, God said that the kingdom would be in ruins 'until he comes to whom it rightfully belongs; to him I will give it' (Ezekiel 21:27 RSV). There was no other Davidic king on the throne after the exile.

Another prediction of the ruin had been made some 150 years earlier, when the Davidic monarchy was still secure on the throne. Isaiah introduced a description of the wise and just rule of the coming king, saying 'A shoot will come up from the stump of Jesse; from his roots a Branch will bear fruit' (Isaiah 11:1 NIV), the stump here being David's father Jesse. When the king came, the line of David would be in a low state, like the stump of a felled tree.

The point was taken. Although there was no apparent indication of a Davidic ruler, the Jewish scholars declared, when asked, that the Scriptures, our Old Testament, showed that the Messiah, the Christ, would be the Son of David (Matthew 22:41-42).

There is one technical point which needs clearing up. The prophecies foretold that the Messiah would come from the line of David. But the two genealogies in Matthew 1 and Luke 3 both trace the line of David to Joseph; and Joseph was not the father of Jesus, although he became legal head of the family.

The simplest explanation is that the genealogy in Luke 3 is that of Mary, since the early chapters of Luke's Gospel are clearly written from Mary's point of view. In Luke, Joseph is the son of Heli, whereas in Matthew's Gospel he is described as the son of Jacob.

Let us suppose, then, that Mary's father was Heli. Mary had a sister; we are told that 'standing by the cross of Jesus were his mother, and his mother's sister' (John 19:25 RSV).

We are nowhere told of a brother. If therefore Heli had two daughters only, the line, which was always traced through the male line, would have died out.

The regulations quoted in Numbers 27:1-11 and 36:1-9 were that when daughters only survived, their possessions and their family name required a male relative, or at least someone of the same tribe, to carry them on. Even if Joseph was not a distant relative of Mary, he was of the line of David, and in marrying her he carried on the line of Heli, thus becoming the son of Heli.

2. The Coming King would be the Son of Man from heaven. The Hebrew *Son of* in similar contexts means 'member of a group'; thus 'sons of the prophets' means 'members of the prophetic order' – and 'Son of Man' means 'man', or more precisely, 'human-being', or 'member of mankind.' (The Greek here does not use the word for man that is tied to the masculine gender.)

We are familiar with the way in which in the Gospels Jesus often uses the title Son of Man for himself. He evidently links the title with its use in Daniel 7. Daniel had a vision of brute nations domineering the earth. The scene changes to heaven, where the Ancient of Days takes his seat on the throne and condemns the brute nations. Then Daniel sees:

'One like a son of man, coming with the clouds of heaven. He approached the Ancient of Days and was led into his presence. He was given authority, glory and sovereign power; all peoples, nations and men of every language worshipped him. His dominion is an everlasting dominion that will not pass away.'

When Daniel asks for the meaning of the vision, he is

told that when the four beast kingdoms are broken, 'the holy people of the Most High shall receive the kingdom, and possess the kingdom for ever.'

When the high priest put Jesus on oath to tell the court 'if you are the Christ, the Son of God', Jesus accepted his statement with the traditional, 'Yes, it is as you say.' He continued by paraphrasing the words of Daniel's vision. 'In future you will see the Son of Man sitting at the right hand of the Mighty One and coming on the clouds of heaven.' To the high priest this was the supreme blasphemy (Matthew 26:63-65).

We should notice two more points about Daniel's vision. The Son of Man succeeds the fourth empire, which is Rome, although this empire is not to be destroyed immediately (Daniel 7:12).

When the vision is interpreted, the figure of the Man is blended with his people. He comes to set up a kingdom centred on himself, and indeed the New Testament declares that he has made 'us to be a kingdom' (Revelation 1:6). Undeniably, the title Son of Man emphasises Christ's genuine humanity; but his words to the high priest also indicate something more.

3. The one who should come would be a very great sufferer, who would lay down his life for the sins of mankind. It is true that this person is never actually called the Messiah in the Old Testament, and it is debatable whether before the coming of Jesus Christ the Jews recognized him under this description.

Once more we must accept the word of Jesus himself for this identification when he spoke of the fulfilment of the words, 'He was numbered with the transgressors' as he went to the cross, and 'bore the sin of many' (Luke 22:37; Isaiah 53:12).

One can hardly blame the Jewish scholars for not recognizing how three apparently contradictory descriptions could be brought together – a human descendant from David, a pre-existing being from heaven, and a dying Servant of God. This is a Bible mystery which hindsight helps us to solve in the person of Jesus Christ. In the same way, we ourselves find it hard to bring together all that is written about his Second Coming, but one day we shall understand.

There is perhaps one hint that might have helped. Zechariah, speaking of the worldwide ruler, describes how he will be 'gentle and riding on a donkey' (Zechariah 9:9-10). Humility is his crowning mark.

We find the Servant of the Lord described in vivid terms in the well-known passages in Isaiah 42:1-7; 49:1-7; 50:4-9; 52:13 to 53:12 and 61:1-4. Some scholars have applied these verses to the nation of Israel; but the Old Testament never regards the nation as sinless, yet the Servant is sinless. Others have identified the Servant with an inner nucleus of Israel who suffer for others, although there is no record in history or in the Prophets of any such group.

Since the verses are so personal, and since they fit perfectly what we know of Jesus in the New Testament, it is only sensible to accept the mystery, and understand the words as applying to him.

If we single out certain points, we see him like a root out of dry ground (Isaiah 53:2), linking him with the descendants of David, who comes like a shoot from a felled stump, from humble surroundings (11:1). He was despised and rejected by the men who counted, such as the Pharisees, who saw no beauty in him (52:2-3). He was brutally treated before his death (52:14; 53:4-5).

When he died he seemed to be deserted by God (53:4). Yet in fact his death was the way of redemption, since he was wounded for our transgressions, and the Lord laid on him the iniquity of us all (53:5-6,12). Instead of his being buried in the criminals' grave prepared for him, he was in the event buried in a rich man's grave (53:9). It seems as if Isaiah was transported in time to the evening of the crucifixion, but is shown the coming resurrection, since in the future the sufferer will see his spiritual offspring, and will prolong his days and will see the fruit of his work (Isaiah 53:10-11).

We have to read Isaiah 53 alongside the Gospel account of the passion story. The other passages speak in more general terms of the Servant's commission, and his complete obedience. He is the new Israel who fulfils what the nation of Israel failed to achieve (Isaiah 49:3), and several times he is seen as not only a blessing to Israel, but a blessing to the whole world (Isaiah 42:4,6; 49:6).

It would be tempting to list here all the remarkable prophecies concerning the Messiah (and they are remarkable). But it is worth a special look at Psalm 22, which was in the mind of Jesus when he quoted the opening words on the cross, 'My God, my God, why hast thou forsaken me?' (RSV).

Whatever David may have understood when he was inspired by God to write this psalm, he was clearly writing 'as Jesus'. The central section describes the mockery of the Jewish leaders, Jesus' physical agony, the piercing of his hands, or wrists[*], and feet, and the dividing up of his garments.

The final ten verses express his confidence in the time to come, when he will proclaim his deliverance to the peoples of the world. Thus, as in Isaiah 53, his death is followed by resurrection, and others who die will find life in God through him. It is indeed a great Bible mystery.

---

[*] In both biblical Hebrew and New Testament Greek there is only a single word for hand and wrist, and a single word for foot and ankle, hence the various interpretations in art showing the position of the nails. This wording is not unique in languages. In modern Russian there is no word for hand. It is part of the whole arm.

Postscript

Looking back over what I have written about miracles and other mysterious events in the Bible, I can foresee three criticisms.

First, that I have been uncritical in my too ready acceptance of the Bible stories. I owe my conversion at Cambridge to an uncritical acceptance of what the Bible says. I accepted the promises of Jesus Christ without having to work out whether he actually said the words or not. Then I spent some forty years, almost the whole of my ordained ministry, on the staff of theological colleges, and lectured for various examinations up to university level. For these I had to keep up to date with the works of both conservative and liberal biblical scholars. I know the reasons for explaining away the plain sense of every one of the 'mysteries', but the reasons for accepting them strike me as far stronger.

So as a result of my teaching ministry I have come to a critical, and not uncritical, acceptance of what the Bible says in doctrine and fact, because it makes sense to my intellect as well as my heart. I doubt whether anyone has

CHRISTIANS AND THE SUPERNATURAL

found this book uncritical in its comments.

The second criticism could be that I have treated the Bible as a puzzle book, with a set of mysteries in it to be solved. In fact, the mysteries of the Bible are few and far between. But as stated earlier, the miracles of the Bible mostly happened in three significant periods:

In bringing his people out of Egypt and into the Promised Land, God demonstrated his power through miracles which met each need as it arose.

Again, when God was launching the era of speaking to his people through the 'still, small voice' of prophecy, he authenticated this fresh plan through miracles, in the time of the prophets Elijah and Elisha.

The third era is the time of Jesus Christ, the promised Messiah, and of the early church which he founded. This is, of course, the climax of God's revelation, and all the history and mysteries are simply steps on the way.

It would be a pity if any reader missed the theme, and did not himself or herself become involved in one of the greatest mysteries: forgiveness and cleaning away of sin, and the new eternal life through personal trust in our Lord Jesus Christ – Saviour, Lord and God.

The other criticism could be that I have at times substituted psychism [psychic phenomena] for God.

I have assumed that while there are some occasions when God has acted directly, he normally works through our natural capacities. We put ourselves in God's hands for the day, and we look to him to use us, and to strengthen the powers that he has given us. Sometimes he enables us to do far more than we could have done unaided.

All that I have tried to show in this book is that some of the mysteries are along the lines of known psychic experiences, although they go beyond mere psychism. In attributing the event to God, the Bible is not eliminating man. Just as God used Samson's strength, and augmented it, so I believe he used latent psychic powers in Elisha, Daniel and other men.

The important point is that none of the events are mere psychic experiments like those attempted today under laboratory conditions. Nor do they represent the exercise of psychic powers for personal gain. Each was and is one more step towards God's preparation for the great day of the Messiah's coming in his incarnation, and his future return in glory at the end of the age.

The Bible is more than the record of the religious ideas of one small nation. It is the steady, ongoing revelation of the one God, Father, Son and Holy Spirit, to whom be glory for ever.

Bibliography

Some books have been mentioned in the various chapters as I referred to them, but there are of course more. Every public library contains books on parapsychology and psychic matters. Very few are written from a specifically Christian standpoint, but one can distinguish between the facts and the author's interpretation. Here are some that should prove helpful for anyone wanting to study further.[*]

1. Christian books

My own two relevant books are out of print, but are in some libraries.

What is Man? (Marshall, Morgan and Scott, 1955); published in America with small revisions as *Man in the Process of Time*, (Eerdmans, 1956); revised as *Mind, Man and the Spirits,* (Paternoster, 1968).

---

[*] The publications mentioned here are of necessity those that were available to the author at the time of publication of the original books. I have not presumed to update this list.

Christianity and the Occult, (Scripture Union 1971). Revised as *Understanding the Supernatural,* (Scripture Union, 1977), and included in this volume by White Tree Publishing in abridged form, along with an abridged version of *Our Mysterious God,* Marshalls, 1984.
Mysteries, John Allan (Lion, 1981). A listing of strange phenomena, with a Christian assessment.

The Christian and the Supernatural, Morton T. Kelsey (Search, 1976).

The Occult; a Christian View, Roger Palms (Oliphants, 1972). Two excellent summaries.

Believe It Or Not, E. Garth Moore (Mowbray, 1977). A balanced assessment.

Christianity or Superstition, Paul Bauer (Marshall, Morgan & Scott, 1966). Very full outlines.

There is often relevant material in publications of the *Churches' Fellowship for Psychical and Spiritual Studies*[*], but [at the time of writing – 1984] I am not happy with the way some of their writers try to evade the biblical condemnation of mediums, which I have taken up in this book.

I think the only Christian writer who has made a close and critical study of Astrology [at the time of writing – 1984] is Dr Anthony P Stone. His two books are drawn from his experience with astrology in India, but he has told me that he hopes to write another now that he has returned to live in England. His books are *Hindu Astrology* (Select Books, India, 1981), which is large and technical, and *Light on Astrology* (Gospel Literature Service, 1979) which is a useful paperback.

---

[*] The *Christian Parapsychologist* was first published September 1975 and is still being published at the time of the publication of this book – 2011.

2. General books

Phenomena, John Michell & Robert Rickard (Thames & Hudson, 1979). This sets out such evidence as there is for almost every strange phenomenon that is alleged to have occurred. Excellent.

A weekly publication in 157 parts, *The Unexplained,* (Orbis Publishing, 1980-83) may be in some libraries in its 13 bound volumes [and single volumes can often be found on eBay]. It is a balanced assessment, for and against, of strange phenomena. [This was written for the poplar market, and subsequent research has changed some of the conclusions, and it would need to be read with caution].

Supernature, Lyall Watson (Hodder & Stoughton, Coronet, 1973). An important and evidential book, often quoted. Subtitled *A Natural History of the Supernatural.*

Explaining the Unexplained, Hans Eysenck and Carl Sargent (Weidenfeld & Nicolson, 1982).

Mind over Matter, Kit Pedler (Thames Television &Methuen, 1981). These last two books are scientific and experimental.

Psi and the Consciousness Explosion, Stuart Holroyd (Bodley Head, 1977). A quiet and thoughtful approach.

3. Older books from libraries

Supernormal Faculties in Man, Eugene Osty (Methuen, 1923). Practical researches by a French doctor, translated from the French.

Occult Phenomena in the Light of Theology, Alois Wiesinger (Burns & Oates, 1957). A remarkable book on human psychic faculties by a Roman Catholic abbot, translated from the German.

The Physical Phenomena of Mysticism, S. J. Thurston (Burns& Oates, 1952). An evidential and open-minded book on physical phenomena ascribed to some of those recognised as saints by the Roman Church.

The *Journals* and *Proceedings* of the Society for Psychical Research are in some libraries, and contain evidential material.

Index

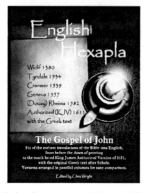

MARY JONES AND HER BIBLE

AN ADVENTURE BOOK

Mary Jones saved for six years to buy a Bible of her own. In 1800, when she was 15, she thought she had saved enough, so she walked barefoot for 26 miles (more than 40km) over a mountain pass and through deep valleys in Wales to get one. That's when she discovered there were none for sale!

You can travel with Mary Jones today in this book by following clues, or just reading the story. Either way, you will get to Bala where Mary went, and if you're really quick you may be able to discover a Bible just like Mary's in the market!

The true story of Mary Jones has captured the imagination for more than 200 years. For this book, Chris Wright has looked into the old records and discovered even more of the story, which is now in this unforgettable account of Mary Jones and her Bible. Solving puzzles is part of the fun, but the whole story is in here to read and enjoy whether you try the puzzles or not. Just turn the page, and the adventure continues. It's time to get on the trail of Mary Jones!

A true story with optional puzzles.
(Some are easy, some tricky, and some amusing.)
Published by Christian publishers White Tree Publishing
ISBN 978-0-9525956-2-5
5.5 x 8.5 inches paperback
UK £6.95, €8.95, US $12.95
156 pages of story, photographs, line drawings and puzzles.
The full story of Mary Jones's and her Bible
with a clear Christian message.

Lightning Source UK Ltd.
Milton Keynes UK

178593UK00001B/5/P